# OUR ETERNAL HOMES.

BY

A BIBLE STUDENT.

"To the law and the testimony: if they speak not according to this word, *it is* because *there is* no light in them." — *Isa.* viii. 20.

"Thy kingdom come."

FROM THE FOURTH LONDON EDITION.

BOSTON:
T. H. CARTER AND SON.
CHICAGO: E. B. MYERS AND CHANDLER.
1866.

University Press: Welch, Bigelow, & Co.,
Cambridge.

TO

THE EVER CHERISHED MEMORY

OF MY MOST TENDER FRIEND AND EARLIEST TEACHER,

MY BELOVED MOTHER,

WHOM IT HAS PLEASED THE DIVINE MERCY TO REMOVE FROM THE CARES,
TOILS, SORROWS, AND ANXIETIES OF EARTH,

THIS LITTLE WORK,

ON A SUBJECT WHICH SHE DELIGHTED TO CONTEMPLATE,

IS MOST GRATEFULLY INSCRIBED

BY

THE AUTHOR.

# CONTENTS.

## INTRODUCTION.



## I.

## WHAT IS HEAVEN?

## II.

## GUARDIAN ANGELS.



## III.

## HEAVENLY SCENERY.

## IV.

### DEATH THE GATE OF LIFE.



## V.

### DO THE DEPARTED FORGET US?



## VI.

### MAN'S BOOK OF LIFE.

# OUR ETERNAL HOMES.

## INTRODUCTION.

VOYAGERS to a distant port, travellers to a far-off country, emigrants from a land of destitution to a land of hope, desire to know somewhat of the character of their several destinations. This desire is not unnatural. Indeed, we should reasonably consider indifference as an indication and a proof of strange shallowness of thought or of feeling. The warmer the hopes that point to that far-off resting-place, the keener will be the anxiety to learn all that can be known as to that resting-place. Delight in contemplating its prospects may be measured by the disposition to inquire into its character. Men, as reasonable beings, must necessarily prefer to investigate most those subjects that take the strongest hold upon their interest. We think the most constantly of that which we love best, and desire to obtain information thereon, to enable us the more fully to think of it. So far from this being unnatural, it is the very necessity of our rational nature; and as such, anxiety to learn something about heaven is at once God-designed and God-given.

Nor is such a disposition puerile. The immensity of human interests that are involved in the subject, — the universal certainty of death, the many dear friends whom we have had, and who are now deceased, gone out from our sight, yet not faded from our memories nor our love, the pregnant questions of immortality and our future life, — all these unite to press the consideration upon us. The strongest minds bow in weakness before the shadows that loom up from the abyss, and become the most absorbed in the contemplation of the secrets of the hereafter. Sage and saint have acknowledged the sovereignty which this anxiety to know has swayed over them; and the tenderest affections which they have cherished have only invested such anxiety with the halos of love. There is so startling a disproportion between our capacities for learning and our opportunities here for acquiring knowledge; between our faculties of use and the occasions afforded on earth for their exercise, that involuntarily all good men seek in the belief of future existence the prospect of a wider arena for sublime action, and an interminable opportunity for acquisition and development. Warped by hope to the contemplation of the future life, we combine with our belief of it the loftiest aspirations and the largest thoughts. It is the glory and pride of man that alone of all animated creatures he is the heir of immortality, and that the rational existence which he possesses fits him to appreciate, and therefore to receive, capacitates him to improve, and therefore to enjoy, perpetual being; and surely it is not improper that he should seek to ascertain somewhat in relation to this sublime prerogative, which marks him the apex of the pyramid of creation, the grand middle term of life, "midway 'twixt nothing and Deity."

While this disposition is neither unnatural nor puerile, it is not unlawful. The best evidence of its lawfulness will be afforded in the proof that it has pleased our Divine Teacher to reveal in His holy word occasional glimpses of heaven and man's future state. Intelligence is the faculty of perceiving, and revelation is the presentation of something to be seen, and which in its absence either could not have been seen at all, or which could not have been seen so clearly. But the very fact that something is revealed, proves that this something was intended by the Revealer to be seen by those to whom the revelation has come. The revelation is the evidence of the intention. Not only to be seen, but also to be investigated; for investigation is only the effort to see more clearly. If it has pleased God to reveal any information on this subject, it is not only not unlawful to endeavor to learn, but further, it is treating the revelation with improper inconsiderateness if we do not endeavor to learn. It must be indeed a slight and an offence to the Communicator to regard with indifference the communication which it has pleased Him to make.

"As is moonlight unto sunlight," so is the light of nature to the light of revelation on all subjects connected with man's immortality or the nature of his hereafter. Poets and philosophers have obtained some dim perception that the cradle and the grave are not the boundaries of human being, that the light kindled at birth is not to be extinguished in the sepulchre, that while the clods of the valley may cover man's body, yet the deathless principle with which he is endowed must and will rise into broader development and grander existence, when the Power that adjoined it to the exquisite machinery of the body shall beckon it away; yet their perception of these sublime facts has been a hazardous conjecture, vague in its character, and ephemeral in its influence on their conduct. It has been rather an intuition than a solid decision of their judgment, a creature of hope more than a child of conviction. The few heathens who held it, so held it despite the ridicule of many, and the stolid incredulity of most. Lord Macaulay only expressed what must more or less be the conviction of a large number of serious and reflecting readers, when he remarks: "In truth, all the philosophers, ancient and modern, who have attempted, without the aid of revelation, to prove the immortality of man, from Plato down to Franklin, appear to us to have failed deplorably." Into the midst of the crude fancies, gross superstitions, vacillating hopes, and the dim mass of uncertainties which existed, revelation comes down like a giant among pigmies, or like a sage among children, to correct their errors and increase their knowledge. It rises like a sun upon the mists and darkness that preceded it, confounding problems and displaying certainties, in order that men may see, where previously they doubted, and understand, where before they laid their hands upon their mouths, having no answer from God.

Guided by the light of nature alone, the hazardous and intricate inductions of reason formed no more than an uncertain pathway for human thought; but by the light of revelation man is safely shown the truth. That God has revealed anything on the subject of heaven is the great proof that He designs us to be instructed. But we can only be instructed by the knowledge so far as we comprehend it, and we can only comprehend so far as we investigate and consider it. Investigation into such subjects cannot therefore be unlawful.

Such investigations are not only lawful; they are highly beneficial. The hope of the Christian lays hold on heaven. The clearer his conviction that heaven is a certainty, and the more vivid his conception of what heaven is, the more potent and operative will be his hope of attaining it. We need not fear that familiarizing his mind with the subject will generate in man either indifference or contempt. The more intimately we know God's works in the natural universe, the more profound becomes our consciousness of His majesty, and the deeper grows our adoration. Similar results must follow a clearer perception of what heaven is. We need not be apprehensive that heaven will exhibit less wisdom, or display less goodness, either in its design or its government, than does the natural universe. Intended to be the everlasting habitation of rational and holy intelligences, it will and must be found to be worthy of God, who has provided it, as well as worthy of man, for whom it has been prepared. Indeed, as heaven is an advanced state, into which the blots that mar and disfigure our earth-life, the strange and problematic blending of evil with good, of pain with pleasure, of misery with happiness, of sorrow with joy, can never enter, — so we may anticipate that heaven will yield testimonies more invariable and still more triumphant to the love and wisdom of our august Creator. These will reward the effort of investigation, and repay its toil. There must be something radically shallow and wrong in our conception of heaven, if we dread the results of a more intimate acquaintance with its nature, or a fuller consideration of its character. Remoteness can only augment uncertainty; but the glories of the future state of the blessed can only shine the more resplendently the more closely we approach them.

Devotion can thereby only find new reasons to rejoice in hope, and to persevere in the pilgrimage of the regenerate life ; while even cursory curiosity may, from contemplation, meet with a new inducement to holiness, or a fresh incentive to deter man from sin. Our inquiries into the mysterious problems of man's earth-life, which now often baffle our limited knowledge, may, perhaps, receive some illustration from a clearer insight into the relation of our present to our future state of existence. Seeing two terms of the problem may aid us in attaining a closer approximation to the solution; and an enlarged comprehension of the *curricula* of heaven may shed light on the probationary processes of earth. That is, man's destiny may irradiate man's wayfaring, and the triumph provided may illume the mysteries of the warfare. The ridicule of scepticism and the objections of infidelity may find a fresh refutation in the evidences our investigation may furnish us of heaven's adaptation to man's highest nature, and the adaptability of man's highest nature to such a heaven as the Bible reveals.

Even though incredulous intellect be but remotely affected, yet the operation of more certain and worthy conceptions of heaven on the *hearts* of believers must be incalculable in its benefits: and so far as the heart can influence the head, and the affections the intellect, even *mind* must be the gainer. The heart of the mourner, blistered with tear-drops at the loss of the beloved, may find from such contemplation an additional consolation. The waning strength of the struggling combatant in temptation may receive through such suggested recollections new power to fight the fight and press forward toward the mark of the prize of our high calling in Christ Jesus our Lord. The bewildered wanderer in the labyrinths of life may obtain direction and a guide, from brighter perceptions of the hereafter ; while the wayworn and weary may be nerved with renewed resolution, as they catch the gleam of the hill-set city nearer to them than they thought. As the sight of home brightens on the heart of the traveller, though mists be mantling round his path, so will clear conceptions of heaven illume and cheer the soul walking Zionwards, which has already decided that in heaven is his home.

In our inquiry into this sublime subject, we shall only seek to learn and indicate the glimpses of heaven furnished to us in the Bible. From the Scriptures we derive our knowledge of the fact that there is such a state. No means other than revelation could supply us with the declaration of this fact. Reason might attain to the induction that such a state *may* exist, as it can show, after the revelation has been afforded, that the declaration is not contrary to our otherwise acquired knowledge. It may thus endeavor, not only to comprehend, but also .to confirm what has been thus made known ; but for the clew and the intimation reason is indebted to revelation. As revelation alone informs us of the fact, revelation alone must supply us with information on the subject. Devout inquirers, we shall attempt only to follow where God in the Bible leads us, and shall discover that as God requires no blind acquiescence in His truth, so He has revealed sufficient to supply reason with its worthiest exercise, together with abundance to satisfy the heart. We shall attempt to draw no conclusions that are not plainly involved in the suggestive words of Holy Writ. God intends not that man should serve Him with an unthinking obedience, or love Him with an irrational devotion; belief in His word is the triumph of reason, and trust in His promises is the culmination of confidence. One thing we shall find, that everything revealed on the subject of heaven is pregnant with practical importance, and potent with application to the daily issues of life. To His service we commend this little book, as for His glory we have written it, in the spirit of the prayer: —

> "What in me is dark,
> Illumine; what is low, raise and support;
> That to the height of this great argument,
> I may assert eternal Providence,
> And justify the ways of God to man."

In so far as the opinions advanced in this little book are novel, we solicit for them attentive consideration; in so far as they are peculiar, we only ask that they be not charged upon others; in so far as they are good in their purpose and tendency, we hope that they will be cherished, and that no idiosyncrasies of thought may frustrate whatever spiritual advantage they might otherwise impart; in so far as they are imperfect, fragmentary, and unsatisfactory, we plead our own deficiencies and ignorance; but in so far as those opinions are in accordance with reasonable deduction, we require for them candor; and in so far as they are consonant with the inspired declarations of the sacred word of God, we demand for them acceptance. "To the law and to the testimony: if they speak not according to this word, it is because there is no light in them." (Isa. viii. 20.)

# I.

## WHAT IS HEAVEN?

"There is one glory of the sun, and another glory of the moon, and another glory of the stars: for one star differeth from another star in glory." — 1 COR. xv. 41.

HEAVEN CONSIDERED AS A STATE, WHAT IT IS, AND BIBLE REFERENCES TO IT. — THE IMPORTANCE OF SO CONSIDERING HEAVEN. — HEAVEN CONSIDERED AS A PLACE. — WHERE IS HEAVEN? — HEAVEN CONSIDERED AS HOME. — VARIETY IN HEAVEN. — PLURALITY OF HEAVENS. — THE THREE GLORIES. — THE NATURAL AND THE SPIRITUAL MEANING OF THE WORD "HEAVEN." — THE ANALOGY OF THE SOUL WITHIN THE BODY TO THE SPIRITUAL WITHIN THE NATURAL UNIVERSE. — "BEYOND THE BOUNDS OF TIME AND SPACE" CONSIDERED. — THE NEARNESS OF HEAVEN PROVED BY THE APPEARANCES OF ANGELS AS RECORDED IN THE BIBLE. — THE TWO COMMONLY RECEIVED HYPOTHESES AS TO THOSE APPEARANCES. — A THIRD STATED, ILLUSTRATED, AND ENFORCED. — WHAT CONSTITUTED A SEER. — MOSES IN THE MOUNT. — THE SPIRITUAL WORLD NOT DISTANT, AS SHOWN IN THE EXPERIENCES OF THE DYING. — TRANCES. — SPIRIT-MANIFESTATIONS CONSIDERED IN THIS CONNECTION. — OBJECTIONS TO PURSUING THE INVESTIGATION EXAMINED AND REFUTED. — THE NEARNESS OF HEAVEN THE SECRET OF STRENGTH. — HEAVENLY TEACHERS. — THE NEARNESS OF HEAVEN THE SECRET OF LIFE. — THE NEARNESS OF HEAVEN THE SECRET OF PRESERVATION. — ALL THE UNIVERSE BOUND TOGETHER IN CONSEQUENCE OF THE NEARNESS OF HEAVEN.

THERE are two modes of considering the question, What is Heaven? First, what constitutes Heaven? or heaven considered as a *state;* and secondly, what is Heaven? or heaven considered as a place.

The Bible frequently treats of heaven as a *state*

of existence, irrespective of the external place where they who are in this heavenly state may objectively dwell. It is in this sense that we are able to understand all that is said of "the kingdom of heaven," or "the kingdom of God." The Lord declared to His disciples that "the kingdom of God cometh not with outward show," for "the kingdom of God is within you,"[1] thus intimating that the heavenly kingdom was a state of holiness and joy, of peace and light, into which His disciples might enter, by its having entered into them. Hence the testimony, "Repent, for the kingdom of heaven is at hand":[2] hence, also, the promise, "Blessed are the poor in spirit, for theirs *is* the kingdom of heaven";[3] theirs not only as a future gift, but also as a present possession: hence, too, the blessing, "Unto you it is given to know the mysteries of the kingdom of heaven, but unto those who are *without*, all these things are done in parables":[4] to the disciples it is given to know the mysteries, because they are *within* the kingdom of heaven, but unto those *without* the kingdom it is not given, because they are *without:* hence, likewise, the gift to the Apostles, that "Whatsoever they should bind on earth should be bound in heaven, and whatsoever they should loose on earth should be loosed in heaven";[5] because the Apostles bearing the truths of the Gospel to the world were the types of those Gospel truths,

1 Luke xvii. 20, 21.
2 Matt. iii. 2.
3 Matt. v. 3.
4 Mark iv. 11.
5 Matt. xviii. 18.

which truths they are that bind and loose the states of man, either confirming him in evil or awakening him to righteousness. Hence also the condemnation of the Pharisees and scribes, "Woe unto you, scribes and Pharisees, hypocrites! for ye shut up the kingdom of heaven against men: for ye neither go in yourselves, neither suffer ye them that are entering to go in."[1] By withholding the precious things of God's word, by making God's commands of none effect by their traditions, by breaking the law and teaching men so, they, in their conduct and by their example, placed impediments in the way of men receiving the precious truths of the kingdom of heaven, and consequently prevented men from realizing that heavenly state of spiritual holiness and peace.

In like manner, the Lord speaks of "the kingdom of God," where in His parables He likens it to many things, and declares the entrance into that kingdom of even harlots, publicans, and sinners, or promises, "That there be some of them that stand here who shall not taste of death, till they have seen the kingdom of God come with power";[2] or asserts to the scribe who had kept the law, "Thou art not far from the kingdom of God";[3] or declares that "It is easier for a camel to go through the eye of a needle, than for a rich man to enter into the kingdom of God";[4] or instructs us, that "Except a

1 Matt. xxiii. 13.
2 Mark ix. 1.
3 Mark xii. 34.
4 Matt. xix. 24.

man be born again, he cannot see the kingdom of God."[1] In like manner, the Apostles confirmed "the souls of the disciples, exhorting them to continue in the faith, and that we must through great tribulation enter into the kingdom of God";[2] or, as St. Paul shows, that "the kingdom of God is not in word, but in power";[3] or, as is sublimely testified by St. John, as he heard "the loud voice in heaven saying, Now is come salvation, and strength, and the kingdom of our God, and the power of his Christ: for the accuser of our brethren is cast down, which accused them before our God day and night,"[4] where the casting down of the accuser describes the destruction of all that is false and evil out of the soul of the believer, that the Christian may feel "the answer of a good conscience toward God,"[5] which is the necessary precursor of the coming of the kingdom of God into the soul, the advent of the heavenly state in salvation and strength.

In many cases where a distinction is drawn between the kingdom of Christ and the kingdom of this world, there is made a like reference to heaven, regarded more particularly as a state of holiness and peace, or as composed of those who have entered into such a state on earth, rather than to the kingdom of God as composed of the saved in heaven. Hence the Lord declares, "The Son of man shall send forth his angels, and they shall gather out of

1 John iii. 3.
2 Acts xiv. 22.
3 1 Cor. iv. 20.
4 Rev. xii. 10.
5 1 Pet. iii. 21.

his kingdom all things that offend, and they that work iniquity";[1] and further, that of the increase "of his kingdom there shall be no end";[2] and, "My kingdom is not of this world: if my kingdom were of this world, then would my servants fight, that I should not be delivered to the Jews: but now is my kingdom not from hence";[3] and, "Fear not, little flock, it is the Father's good pleasure to give you the kingdom." The "kingdom and glory of God, unto which the Christian is called,"[4] is the sovereignty of holiness, purity, goodness, truth; the dominion in which the whole man is subject to the laws of the great King; an allegiance owned here, by which they are made not only heirs to "the glory which shall be," but inheritors of the glory that even now is. The glory which shall be is only the consummation and fuller development of the glory already begun here; and the joy begun to be realized here is the foretaste of the joy to be evermore amply realized above. The disciple is already "a child of the kingdom," not merely as sharing the promise, but as already having entered thereinto. The guaranty of his future blessedness is the possession of the present blessedness whereunto he has attained. Holiness is heaven, love is heaven; and the heaven of the future, the objective heaven, can only be a grander embodiment of love and holiness. The importance of this consideration cannot be exaggerated; as neither the Bible nor reason

1 Matt. xiii. 41. 2 Luke i. 33. 3 John xviii. 36. 4 1 Thess. ii. 12.

affords us any ground of presumption that those who have not realized this heaven begun here, can hope to realize the heaven completed hereafter. On heaven as a *state* must all adequate conceptions of heaven as a *place* be founded, and therefore we have presented the former as our first topic of consideration.

Heaven as a place, where are assembled and where dwell the saved ones, "the children of the kingdom," or those in whom the kingdom of God had previously begun on earth, also receives many notices in the Bible. Perhaps the best illustration of heaven which our earth-life affords to us is the idea of HOME. *Home* embraces all we can conceive of peace, of rest, of joy; the presence of the dear ones whose happiness is interblended with our own, the circle of loving services and devoted uses, with God for its great Head, God's word for its chief guide, the fostering and development of goodness and delight in each other as its prime object. And heaven is the idea of home, extended, as to locality, into everlasting habitations, enlarged, as to inhabitants, till it comprehends all God's children; with its peace intensified till it knows no fear, its joy amplified till every tear shall be wiped away from the face, its holiness increased till nothing shall hurt or destroy in all God's holy mountain, with innumerable multitudes on multitudes as ministers of blessing, one to all and all to each. All the lingering attachments which bind our heart to home receive grander measure and profounder depth, in proportion as with our idea of home we associate the fuller idea of heaven, with God as the universal Father, and the saved as our universal brethren. Arguing from the seen to the unseen, from the known to the unknown, which is the only sound method, the idea of *home*, which we know, will enable us to attain a conception of the *heaven*, which we know not yet. In a sense far deeper than our perceptions previously enabled us to utter it, we may say that "our home is in heaven"; for all the various felicities with which the Divine mercy allows our home-life on earth to be environed are only mundane pictures or emblems of the broader and more bountiful bliss which the same Divine mercy has prepared in heaven. Not that the earthly shall be sublimed or intensified into the heavenly; but, with that difference which ever must exist between earth and heaven, the earthly *purest* is still the type of the heavenly *pure*.

Prominent among the descriptions furnished us of heaven is the scriptural assertion of the variety that exists there. Heaven is not to be regarded as an unvarying monotony, either in the place of habitation or in the character of those who dwell there. On the contrary, the idea is repugnant to all that we know of man, and all that, from that knowledge, we may hope for man's future. God has not made two things alike. The unity of God is preserved in the unity of all His works, just as the infinity of God is mirrored in the variety which He has impressed on all His works. As we shall develop this idea elsewhere, we do no more than indicate it here, seeking in this place only to show the scriptural statement of the thought as applied to heaven. The Apostle declares that "there is one glory of the sun, and another glory of the moon, and another glory of the stars: for one star differeth from another star in glory."[1] This threefold distinction of heaven receives confirmation from that other statement made by the same Apostle in his second epistle to the same Church at Corinth: "It is not expedient for me doubtless to glory. I will come to visions and revelations of the Lord. I knew a man in Christ above fourteen years ago, (whether in the body, I cannot tell; or out of the body, I cannot tell: God knoweth;) such a one caught up to the third heaven. And I knew such a man, (whether in the body, or out of the body, I cannot tell: God knoweth;) how that he was caught up into Paradise, and heard unspeakable words, which it is not lawful [or possible] for man to utter: of such a one will I glory."[2] That these words do assert the existence of a plurality of heavens there can be no question, and that they intimate this plurality to consist of three heavens there can be no just reason to dispute. St. Paul is evidently speaking of himself, who, by the Divine mercy, had thus been intromitted into the

[1] 1 Cor. xv. 41. [2] 2 Cor. xii. 1-5.

third heaven. This narrative gives additional weight to the description furnished in his first epistle, wherein he compares the various degrees of the glory of heaven severally to that of the sun, and moon, and stars.

That there should be such a threefold distinction in the heavens is eminently reasonable, when we consider that there are also three grand planes of spiritual life, in each of which thousands of Christians do really exist. Some act from a principle of simple *Obedience.* Because God has *commanded*, they obey; and the predominant idea in their conception of God is as to His Divine *Power.* Others act from love of the *Truth.* Seeing the harmony of the Divine injunctions with their highest wants and noblest nature, their realization of the spirit of Christianity is rather directed to the beauty and excellence of the Divine *Wisdom.* Others again act from the overpowering force of LOVE. The Divine *Goodness* is the supreme object of their contemplation and reverence. These are the "living ones" of the Revelation; they "run and are not weary, walk and are not faint"; the "Garden of the Lord," Eden, is restored to their souls, and the law of the Lord is written on the secret tablets of their hearts. A similar distinction is made in the Bible as to the three orders of angels. Not only is there mention made of the *cherubim*, or guarding ones, and *seraphim*, or flaming ones, in the Old Testament; but the distinction is also still more explicitly made in the Revelation. The "living ones" (wrongly translated *beasts*), "the elders" (the wise ones), and "the ten thousand times ten thousand round the throne."[1] A similar distinction exists in the characters of Peter, all-earnest for faith, and the first to *acknowledge* the Lord Jesus; of James, zealous of good works; of John, into whose soul, as a crystal chalice, the melting draughts of LOVE seem to have been poured. A similar distinction appears to have prevailed in the tabernacle of the wilderness, which was made "after the pattern of things in the heavens,"[2] and which had a court, a holy place, and the Holy of Holies. Thus, with the invariably consistent symbolism of the Bible, repeating this threefold distinction.

This assertion of plurality in relation to heaven derives additional corroboration from the plural form in which heaven is so frequently spoken of elsewhere. Even in the prayer which the Lord taught His disciples to use there is an express assertion of this plurality, although the translators of the Gospels have obliterated it in our version. "After this manner therefore pray ye: Our Father who art in *the heavens*."[3]—ὁ ἐν τοῖς οὐρανοῖς, "*in the heavens*." Thus the Lord has provided that even in our daily prayers we should be reminded of the plurality of the heavens, and their consequent adaptation to every variety of human character, which would ever remain individually distinct, although

[1] Rev. v. 11. [2] Heb. ix. 23. [3] Matt. vi. 9.

harmonized into the whole congregation of the saved, by having undergone, in common with all the redeemed ones, the sanctifying operations of regeneration, and having shared in the purification of the Gospel of Christ. Were it not for these plain statements, we might be inclined to regard as poetical hyperbole the use of the plural *heavens*, in many of the descriptions of the Old Testament; but illustrated by these, every such use of the plural form becomes an additional evidence, so that, instead of being regarded as examples of mere poetical exaggeration, they solidify into assertions of fact. Hence, "Give ear, O ye heavens, for I will speak; and, hear, O earth, the words of my mouth";[1] and, "His heavens shall drop down dew";[2] and, "He bowed the heavens also, and came down: and darkness was under his feet";[3] and, "Yea, the heavens are not clean in his sight";[4] and, "By his Spirit he hath garnished the heavens";[5] and, "Thou hast set thy glory above the heavens";[6] and, "He shall call to the heavens from above, and to the earth, that he may judge his people";[7] and, "Let the heavens rejoice, let the earth be glad,"[8] and, "The heaven, even the heavens, are the Lord's: but the earth shall be given to the children of men";[9] and, "The heaven of heavens cannot contain thee";[10] and, "I have

1 Deut. xxxii. 1.
2 Deut. xxxiii. 28.
3 Ps. xviii. 9.
4 Job xv. 15.
5 Job xxvi. 13.
6 Ps. viii. 1.
7 Ps. l. 4.
8 Ps. xcvi. 11.
9 Ps. cxv. 16.
10 1 Kings viii. 27.

put my words in thy mouth, and I have covered thee in the shadow of mine hand, that I may plant the heavens, and lay the foundation of the earth, and say unto Zion, Thou art my people";[1] and, "Behold, I create new heavens";[2] and, "I will hear the heavens, and they shall hear the earth";[3] and, "For David is not yet ascended into the heavens";[4] and, "Whom the heavens must receive until the times of restitution";[5] and, "We have a High-Priest, that is passed into the heavens";[6] and, "Let us lift up our hearts unto God in the heavens";[7] and, "Unto thee lift I up mine eyes, O thou that dwellest in the heavens";[8] and, "Provide yourselves a treasure in the heavens that faileth not";[9] and, "We have a house not made with hands, eternal in the heavens";[10] besides numerous other passages, all combine to confirm and establish the explicitly declared statement of the plurality of the heavens.

Nor must we confound such declarations with references made to the natural heaven or heavens, the firmament surrounding the earth, in speaking of which the plural form is frequently used, as in, "The heavens declare the glory of God; and the firmament showeth his handiwork."[11] The natural heavens with their glowing galaxies of stars are by analogy often employed to *represent* the spiritual

[1] Isa. li. 16.
[2] Isa. lxv. 17.
[3] Hos. ii. 21.
[4] Acts ii. 34.
[5] Acts iii. 21.
[6] Heb. iv. 14.
[7] Lam. iii. 41.
[8] Ps. cxxiii. 1.
[9] Luke xii. 33.
[10] 2 Cor. v. 1.
[11] Ps. xix. 1.

heavens, the abodes of the blessed; but even while they bear a natural or literal application to the physical heavens, many of the passages evidently refer, in their deeper sense, to the spiritual heavens, the everlasting dwelling-places of the children of God. Indeed, it would furnish a subject full of interest to inquire how the same expression, heaven, became appropriated both to the physical firmament and to the spiritual abodes of the angels; and singularly suggestive reasons might be found to show why, in common with many other expressions, both a physical and psychological, a natural and a spiritual signification have been attached to it. As the physical heaven is at once the highest and most glorious object our natural sight can behold, so the same word is exalted into being the expression of the highest and most glorious object our mental sight can behold; and thus heaven the natural becomes the visible symbol of heaven the spiritual, and which at present remains the invisible. The thought of the spiritual, when concreted into language, is forced to assume terms to which our outward senses have previously affixed only natural meanings; and thus a link of analogy is established between them. This is a necessary result of "wedding thought to speech," of bringing down our higher conceptions into the lower plane of utterance. The ineffable is pictured in the visible, the spiritual is concreted into the natural, soul is embodied, and the body is its effigy and image. This is so, not only as to things, but also as to language. We can, however, do no more here than glance at this interesting subject as we pass it by.

Granting, then, that there is a plurality of heavens, and admitting that this plurality consists of three, the question occurs, Where then is heaven? The first answer is, that heaven is not a natural place, that is, not within the confines of natural space. As heaven is the abode of spiritual beings, so it must be a spiritual place; and if such a definition be difficult of comprehension, it may be asked, where in the body is the soul of man? Some have located it in the whole brain; but there seems but little more reason to assign to it such a locality, than with others, to believe that it resides in the heart, or with others, to conceive of its being exclusively located in the pineal gland. That its connection with the body is established through the subtler energies of the nervous system, and that its more immediate contact with the organism is effected in the brain, there may be reason to believe; but to affix to it a local habitation there, is certainly presuming too far. As the spiritual being, the soul, is within the body and yet not of it, so heaven may be regarded as being within nature and yet not of it. It is beyond the bounds of space, not as being situated in some indescribable region far beyond the physical stars, but as being uncircumscribed by the limitations of physical space; just as it is beyond the bounds of time, in being unfettered with its limitations, and unaffected by its laws.

We must neither look to the sun, as some have done, and fancy that heaven may be there, nor to Sirius, nor to any others of the stars, and believe that heaven may there be found. It is spoken of as "the invisible world," just as man's spirit may be regarded as *the invisible man*, — a spiritual world at present hidden from us, because our present perceptions are almost entirely *natural*, yet neither distant as to locality, nor remote as to time. Near to us as the spirits of other human beings are near to us, and as our spirit is near to them, and yet possessing a contiguity that is not to be measured by feet and furlongs.

To this conclusion all the Scripture declarations abundantly tend. We will adduce a few of the many testimonies furnished in the Bible.

The Apostle John is in the isle of Patmos, and "on the Lord's day," as he informs us, "he was in the spirit." As to his body, he was a convict on the island, and yet he beheld the world of spirits, — the middle state, into which the souls of men first enter after the death of the body, — also heaven, and a still higher heaven, out of which the New Jerusalem descended. He saw myriads of the saved, "out of every nation, tribe, tongue, and people"; conversed with angels, with the elders, — the holy ones; and heard the awful voice of God. Three hypotheses are before us, by which to account for this marvellous apocalypse. One is, that the whole revelation was a vision, or a series of visions, that is, nothing more than a series of ideas presented before the Apostle's mind. When he asserts that he SAW, we should, according to this theory, read, "he *imagined that he saw*"; and when he avers that he HEARD, we ought to understand "he *thought that he heard*"; that though it seemed to him as if he did really both hear and see, yet it was all a mental process, a set of hallucinations providentially appointed and arranged, but entirely subjective in their nature, without there being any corresponding objective realities. This hypothesis shocks our veneration for the Word of God; it altogether shakes our confidence in the accounts of the appearances of angels contained in the Bible, and it lends weight to Paine's objection,—"When it is said that Joseph saw an angel in a dream, it only means that he dreamed that he saw an angel." Every argument on the immortality of the soul, and every illustration of man's future state of existence drawn from such experiences as those of John, have all their foundations swept away by the adoption of this hypothesis. Such experiences would then prove nothing beyond the existence of the individual experiencing them, and would be the high-road to Berkleyism and nothingness.

If the mind recoils from such a conception and its consequences, there is, however, another hypothesis; although this is but very little more satisfactory. It is that angels and spirits were permitted to assume a temporary covering of something resembling human bodies, so that they might for a time be rendered visible to the natural senses of the seers. This rescues us, truly, from the dangers of the theory above noticed; but while it requires the performance of a most remarkable and astounding miracle on every occasion when angels or spirits appeared, it likewise tends to undermine and destroy a lively faith in the reality and objectivity of heaven, or the spiritual world. Even more insidious than the before-mentioned hypothesis, it does not even spiritualize the seers, but it for a time carnalizes the angels. Grant this view, and for aught we know, spiritual beings, when not temporarily invested with a visible and objective substance, may be formless, aerial nothings, — an idea utterly bewildering to human thought to conceive of, provocative of no wish to become like them, and only subversive of love of heaven, or the desire to enter therein.

There is yet another hypothesis which may be entertained, and which avoids the *Scylla* and *Charybdis* of both the above.

It is that the spiritual world is so contiguous to man that it needed no more than the opening of the spiritual senses of the seer, — those senses of which the physical are but the *concretions*, the natural symbols the earthly types, — and, thus empowered to see and hear, that the Apostle did really both hear and see what the Apocalypse declares him to have seen and heard. By this hypothesis the Revelation is rescued from the meiosis of being a mere subjective mental phenomenon, a set of hallucinations, a series of impressions on his imagination, dramatic in form, vividly remembered when he awoke, and afterwards accurately described. It also rescues the vision from the more astounding pretence that it was produced by a species of incarnation of the myriads of spiritual beings whom the Apostle is declared to have seen. The voices that he heard, and the spectacles he beheld, present insuperable difficulties in the way of receiving this last theory; for it would require that the scenes should have been temporarily made *substantial* in this plane of matter in order that he might perceive them, and that the voices should have actually stirred the pulses of the air in order that he might hear them. By the adoption of the third view that we have offered, the Apocalypse becomes an *objective reality*, and the spiritual world is shown to be not very far off.

In confirmation of this, the temptation of Jesus presents similar testimonies. In the wilderness, when fasting and hungry, the Devil is described to have presented himself to tempt Jesus; and when the tempter was subdued, "angels ministered unto him."[1] This leads us again to the conclusion of

[1] Matt. iv. 11.

the contiguity of the spiritual world. So, again, in the narrative of the transfiguration. Jesus was with Peter, James, and John, on the mountain, "and his face did shine as the sun, and his raiment was white as the light. And Moses and Elias appeared unto them [the disciples] talking with him [Jesus]."[1] In this, the most sublime spectacle ever presented to human sight, it is far more rational to believe in the fact that the disciples were empowered to see by the opening of their spiritual sight, and that thus they really beheld Moses and Elias, than it is to believe either that Moses and Elias temporarily invested themselves with material covering perceptible to the natural sight of the disciples, or that the whole was a phantasmagoria, a hallucination of their senses, a freak of fancy, or a dream of their imaginations. It certainly does appear more in consonance with reason, more in harmony with the other statements of the Bible, and more worthy of God, that such manifestations should be produced by operating the change in the seers, by which they were enabled to see, than that the change should have been wrought in the angels by which they were rendered temporarily visible. And this is eminently confirmed by the fact that in some instances, as in the case of Saul of Tarsus,[2] the perception was confined to one person; all hearing the voice, but Saul alone seeing the Lord: as also in the case of Stephen, who,

[1] Matt. xvii. 23. [2] Acts ix. 7.

surrounded by the infuriate mob, judged by his enemies, and afterwards stoned to death, declared, "I see the heavens opened, and the Son of man standing on the right hand."[1] And this will still more clearly appear from the cases to be cited below.

When Elijah was in the wilderness, weary in spirit, and wishing to die, "angels ministered unto him";[2] and when he was about to depart from this earthly scene of probation, Elisha, who was with him, desired as the last gift of God through his tutor and friend, that "a double portion of his spirit might be upon him." Elijah replied, "Thou hast asked a hard thing: nevertheless, *if thou see me when I am taken from thee*, it shall be so unto thee; but if not, it shall not be so."[3] The answer reads like an enigma, but as explained according to the above hypothesis, it is of easy solution. "When I am taken from thee I shall be surrounded by spiritual beings; I shall have become an inhabitant of the spiritual world; these spiritual beings thou canst not see without the opening of thy spiritual sight, and this power of seeing spiritual beings is God's alone to bestow. If He will bestow this power, it shall be unto thee a sign that thy prayer is answered, that thou art indeed a *seer*, and that my office and my power shall be increased by God in thee." Still "they went on, and talked, and behold, there appeared a chariot

[1] Acts vii. 56. [2] 1 Kings xix. 21. [3] 2 Kings ii. 9, 10.

of fire, and horses of fire, and parted them asunder; and Elijah ascended unto heaven. And Elisha saw it, and cried, My father, my father, the horsemen of Israel, and the chariots thereof."[1] The gift of spiritual sight was conferred, Elijah was thus appointed and acknowledged of God as a *seer*, the prayer was answered, and in more than a natural sense, "the mantle of Elijah descended upon Elisha."[2]

That Elisha retained the possession of this power, that it sustained him in his wanderings, supported him in his dangers, was his comfort and surety, the guaranty to him of his being able to perform his mission, and the source of strong hope, we have a further testimony. The King of Assyria had been baffled by the wisdom of the seer, who warned the King of Israel of his stratagems, and, incensed against Elisha, he sent to Dothan, where the prophet was staying, and encompassed the city with his army. When the "young lad," Elisha's servant, saw the host, he exclaimed, "Alas, my master! how shall we do?" And Elisha answered, "Fear not: for they that be with us are more than they that be with them. And Elisha prayed, and said, Lord, I pray thee, *open his eyes, that he may see.* And the Lord *opened the eyes* of the young man; and he saw: and, behold, the mountain was full of horses and chariots of fire round about Elisha."[3] Here the declara-

[1] 2 Kings ii. 11, 12. [2] 2 Kings ii. 12, 13. [3] 2 Kings vi. 16, 17.

tion is explicit. The angelic guards and companions were round about Elisha; he, the seer, saw them, and did not fear: he, the young man, saw them not, because *his eyes were not opened*, yet they were none the less there. The prayer was that the young man's eyes might be opened; in answer to the prayer, the young man's eyes were opened, and he beheld only what his master had seen previously. Their presence was not affected either by his not seeing, or his being able to see; the change wrought in his sight only effected the change in his perception. Though unseen, the angels were still there, and his seeing them there only revealed to the young man the previously existing fact. As we have in this narrative the fullest description of the mode by which the seeing of angels was conferred on a mortal man, this description may rightly serve to explain all those narratives in which the description is less explicit or copious. From this description, and from all other narratives interpreted by this description, we must therefore conclude that the seeing of angels was effected by the *opening of the eyes* of the beholders, and that therefore the spiritual world is contiguous to us even while we are here. Did angels appear to Abraham, to Hagar, to Jacob, to Moses, to the elders of Israel, to Joshua, to Manoah, to Samuel, to Isaiah, to Ezekiel, to Daniel, to Zechariah, and hosts of others living in the Old Testament times; or to Mary, or Joseph, or Elizabeth, or Zacharias, or Jesus, or the Apostles, the same phenomena were rendered possible to the beholders of them by the same simple, sufficient, universal means, — *their eyes were opened, and they saw.*

The inevitable result of such intercourse with the spiritual world on the minds of those permitted to enjoy it, must have been the creation in them of a conviction that the spiritual world was not remote. Indeed, to a man like Elisha, a seer, the conviction of the nearness of the spiritual world must have grown into a consciousness, which, if not so constantly maintained as his natural consciousness, was equally a matter of certainty which nothing could shake. And in whatever degree the eyes of others of the seers of the Bible were opened, by so many times as they were permitted to gaze into the spiritual world and behold the inhabitants or the things thereof, exactly so many were the demonstrations they received of the contiguity of the spiritual world, and just to that degree of certainty must their convictions have attained that heaven is not far off. To them the expression of heaven being "*upward*," could only suggest the idea, not of physical altitude, but of moral elevation, an altitude not to be measured by degrees and minutes of the circle of the natural universe, but to be meted out according to the higher and nobler standard of holiness and obedience to God. To them God was the Most High, not merely from elevation in space, but from His ineffable Majesty, the infinitude of His Goodness and Wisdom and Greatness; and to ascend nearer to Him was a spiritual approximation to His Goodness and Wisdom and Purity. Thus the physical expression of *upward* was sublimed into being the exponent of a spiritual idea; they could rightly employ no other, and it was adequate to their meaning when correctly understood. However much, therefore, they may have blended in their descriptions of heaven the idea of ascending to, or descending from it, such terms were used rather to express elevation and depression of *state*, than to signify geographical or astronomical altitude. The presence of angels, the vision of spirits, the glorious revelations they enjoyed, were intromissions into an adjoining, though interior, world; a world which they knew to be around them, of which, by their spirits and as to their spirits, they were already inhabitants, though it might be shrouded from their normal conditions, and veiled from those grosser senses which were fitted to take cognizance only of the material substances of earth. In a higher than figurative sense, in a sense, indeed, of full objective truth, the aged Christian, weighed down by years, but buoyant with spiritual hope, may be *nearer to heaven* than when he commenced the pilgrimage of regeneration.[1]

From this broad principle of the contiguity of

[1] Rom. xiii. 11.

the spiritual world we can understand how Moses should see the patterns of the tabernacle in the heavens, while his body was physically present on the mount. St. Paul declares that "it was therefore necessary that the patterns of things in the heavens [the holy places] should be purified with these [sacrifices]; but the heavenly things themselves with better sacrifices than these";[1] for those things which Moses made "serve unto the example and shadow of heavenly things, as Moses was admonished of God when he was about to make the tabernacle: for, See, saith he, that thou make all things according to the pattern showed to thee in the mount."[2] The patterns that Moses saw were things in the spiritual world, into which he was permitted to gaze, while he was, as to his body, on the mount.

Similar is the gleam of light which this principle throws upon the visions of Ezekiel, of the temple, the great river, and the city, new Jerusalem; "The Jerusalem which is above is free, which is the mother of us all."[3] So also with the visions of Zechariah, of Daniel, of John, and, in fine, with all the visions recorded in the Bible; — they were objective realities seen in the spiritual world, into which the seers were intromitted, in order that the Word of God might be written as we have it.

To the vast mass of testimony afforded from

[1] Heb. ix. 23. [2] Heb. viii. 5. [3] Gal. iv. 26.

such sources may be added evidence different in kind, but still confirmatory. There is in human history an unwritten chapter, which is yet thronged with mysterious incidents half fearfully remembered by their witnesses. To publish them might provoke the witless sneers of materialistic satirists, as well as wound the feelings of those of whose feelings the love that we cherish for them makes us most regardful. All who have frequently stood beside the bed of the dying must have been thrilled with singular testimonies that the dying are conscious of the presence of other than mortal visitants. It would be shallow and cruel to assert that the weakening faculties of those passing away were deceived, and that such consciousness was hallucination. Though some may take refuge in this belief, on reflecting upon such incidents, yet *at the moment when the dying utter their testimonies*, it is difficult for even scepticism to doubt. The thrill they feel gives denial to the unbelief they afterwards profess. Is it not a grander and more consolatory conviction, that when Christians are passing away from their earth-work to their eternal homes, then the attenuating links that chain consciousness to time and clay are melting away one by one, and their consciousness becomes, by the gradual enfranchisement of a lingering death, more and more spiritual? Thus sinking to sleep as to earth, they are awaking to heaven; growing unmindful of the lower and outer existence, they are arousing to the inner and spiritual life; becoming blind to the clay-enveloped forms of friends standing round their failing bodies, they see already, as through a mist, the brighter beings who are to be their everlasting companions, — some of whom may be already welcoming their coming. Their hearing waxing dim and unconscious to the melody of beloved voices whispering in their natural ears, they can become aware of a sweeter music sung by more exquisite voices still, of the beloved who have gone before them: in fine, dying unto earth, they are becoming alive unto heaven. Does this not fully and worthily explain the solemn scenes of thousands of death-beds? visions of spiritual visitants ministering to the dying, resplendent light surrounding glorious beings who hardly cast a shadow, gorgeous scenery, bright with never-fading beauty, voices thrilling in tenderness, music mysterious in harmony, the recognition of dear familiar faces fondly loved in the bygones, or the foreknowledge which some have received of the exact moment of their departure? There are few families who have not some tale of this kind to tell, some testimony to add to this proof of the contiguity of the spiritual world. They hide such secrets in their hearts, not caring to provoke the ridicule of the incredulous, and in the feeling that there is something too holy in such reminiscences to permit them to cast them to the dogs. Yet the memories of such incidents still cling to them, perhaps more closely for their silence, and such recollections establish in them the certainty that the other world is nearer to us than many have believed.

To this source of evidence may be added another, — that furnished by the singular phenomenon of trances. The history of such has seldom been fairly written, or if written, hardly credited. Yet this class of proofs deserves to be not entirely overlooked by a thoughtful examiner into the evidences of a future state and the contiguity of the spiritual world. The proof of both is sufficient without it, and at most, the few well-authenticated cases of the kind could only supply corroboration, and, perhaps, illustration of that which, independently of such evidence, must be regarded as so certainly a fact. We only indicate rather than omit it. With this class of evidences may be included those furnished by one of the most extraordinary phenomena of modern times, — spiritism. We cannot deny that amid much imposture and more self-delusion there does appear to be some certainty of spiritual agency in some of their operations. That the spirits who perform in them are of the lowest and most degraded order we think there is no reason to doubt, and that, therefore, herein consists the real danger of all such physical manifestations; but we cannot join in that shallow and easy reprobation of the whole, which denies without due investigation, and which denial is often the result of hastiness, prejudice, and ignorance. So far as spiritism is fictitious, so far it is incapable of supplying evidence for or against anything, except the weakness or wickedness of its practices; but so far as it is genuine, so far certainly it affords a fresh evidence of the fact of a future life, and of the contiguity of the spiritual world to the natural world.

But it may be objected, that if the fact of there existing such a state and place as heaven be admitted, any inquiries into its nature or whereabouts is unnecessary, serving only to gratify a curiosity at best unpractical, and at worst idle. Surely not! It may be because we regard heaven as so far off, that we are so far off from heaven. The conviction of the nearness of heaven increases our sense of its reality. It is invisible; but if felt to be near, it becomes all the more real to our consciousness. The analogy between the invisible soul and the invisible spiritual world being clearly seen, we grow more believing as to its actuality. The spirit is invisible, yet joy is real, and sorrow is real; happiness and heart-break, contentment and repining, peace and remorse, are all real, and from the realities of the invisible soul we may rise to a deeper sense of the realities of the invisible spiritual world. Tears and smiles, laughter and mournfulness, are only the effects produced in the body by the emotions of the spirit: they are the outward signs of our spiritual activities. The cause is felt to be real, if only from the reality of the effects it produces. Sobs and groans, ejaculations and cachinnations, are only the vocal language which the visible body supplies to the sensations of the invisible spirit. Under the pressure of intense thought, or the burden of terrible calamity, the hair has been known to become gray in a night; digestion is impeded, or hunger quelled by hearing disastrous news; paralyzed limbs have become active under the influence of strong excitement; fear has produced syncope and death; faith has wrought its cures, and overwhelming grief has burst the muscular coatings of the heart: the emotions of the invisible soul have wrought such realities in the physical organism to which it is annexed. The conviction of the reality of the soul is increased by these evidences of its immediate presence in the body, and its close connection therewith. In like manner, to prove the nearness of heaven is to strengthen our conviction of its reality. And to strengthen our conviction of its reality is to enable that conviction to operate upon our souls far more effectually as an incentive to holiness, and to deter us from sin.

The nearness of the spiritual world may, further, become the secret of *strength*. The power that has sustained martyrs and even fanatics in their cruel experiences, the power that has supported prophets and even self-deluded impostors, the power that has enabled conquerors of nations and the changers of the face of political affairs to perform their missions among men, the power that has inspired reformers and philanthropists, all those who have discovered nature's arcana, and all those who have developed human progress, — may perhaps be found explained from the contiguity of the spiritual world. The world has its heroes in every department of science, art, jurisprudence, philosophy, literature, mechanics, commerce, and national politics, and the secret of their greatness may be this: — that they were more open to the inflowing of thought into their minds, and heroism into their hearts from the spiritual world than other men, — more capable recipients and apter exponents of spiritual activity going on within them. The fact is, and it is as grand a fact as it is all-embracing, that man is bound about with spiritual ties. We owe the knowledge that we acquire by an external way, partly to the exercise of our powers of observation, but still more to the instructions of men in the flesh who have left us rich legacies of learning; but who can tell for how many of the clear perceptions, the noble purposes, the far-reaching intuitions, the lustrous gleams and glances of thought that visit us in our quiet hours of contemplation, we are indebted to men in the spirit who are with us and near us, as full of love as earthly friends may be, and far abler to guide us to truth, and to influence us for good? The universally asserted afflatus of poetry is more than a figure of rhetoric, a rhapsodical figment, or a pretty fiction. The ablest of writers have admitted that the ideas they have communicated to mankind were rather given to them than originated by them, results of a *reception* rather than a *creation;* and if there be any truth in this opinion, then the nearness of the spiritual world may present us with a key to the mystery.

The nearness of the spiritual world may be the secret of LIFE. God is the sole source of being, and its more immediate recipients must be those who are nearest to Him; and the outflowing streams of life may pass onwards and outwards through the spiritual world into the natural universe, just as the vital power flows from man's soul, as its first recipient from God, the only source of life, into man's body as its physical receptacle and organism. On this topic we forbear to dwell, feeling that here we must take our shoes from off our feet, for this is holy ground.

The nearness of the spiritual world we shall subsequently prove to be a marvellous explanation of the secret of Providence; as we may here see that it will reveal to us the secret of preservation. As life when first communicated is the gift of God, so the preservation of life is the continued impartation of life. The great stream of life from which all things live is exhaustless in quantity, and its impartation is from moment to moment. To cease to receive it for an instant would be to die. Not only have we originally derived our life from God, we also live from God continually. If the heavens, being nearer to God, are the first recipients of life from Him, and from being passive recipients they become active mediums or instrumentalities for the impartation of their derived life to spheres still more remote, then the contiguity of the spiritual to the natural universe will elucidate the preservation of the natural universe. In this way the vast chain of being may be seen to be complete in itself, and comprehending all things; the natural exists, and is preserved from the spiritual, and the spiritual exists, and is preserved immediately from God. With a fuller perception and a juster discrimination than was possessed by Kant, we can now see that the spiritual world is thus, as it were, the soul of the natural universe, and the only source of the life of that soul is God. Just as the body of a man not only lives from the man's soul, but is also preserved by its connection with the soul, so the existence and preservation of the natural world is secured by its connection with, and consequent nearness to, the spiritual world, the glorious places of which are heaven.

Bound together indissolubly as the creatures of one Creator, the children of one Father, men in the natural world and men in the spiritual world are participators in one common brotherhood; and the nearness of heaven is at once the hope and solace, the joy and glory of earth, its mystery of creation and preservation, its source of strength and the secret of its beauty. This may, perhaps, be called mysticism; but it is a mysticism full of comfort and hope to man.

# II.

## GUARDIAN ANGELS.

"For he shall give his angels charge concerning thee, to keep thee in all thy ways" — Ps. xci. 11.

MAN AN INHABITANT OF BOTH THE NATURAL AND THE SPIRITUAL WORLDS. — EVEN WHILE HERE HAS ASSOCIATES IN BOTH. — THE ARGUMENT FROM THE NATURE OF MAN. — THE ARGUMENT FROM THE NATURE OF ANGELS. — ANGELS ARE INTELLIGENT, LOVING, ACTIVE BEINGS, AND POSSESS THE HUMAN FORM. — THE ARGUMENT FROM ANALOGY. — THE ARGUMENT FROM THE BIBLE. — THE PEOPLE OF ISRAEL. — THE NEW TESTAMENT DISPENSATION. — OBJECTIONS CONSIDERED. — THE PROPOSITION OF ANGELIC MINISTRATIONS RIGHTLY STATED. — THE UNIVERSAL DECLARATIONS OF THE SCRIPTURES. — THE CASE OF DANIEL, THE ANGEL, AND THE PRINCES OF PERSIA AND GRECIA. — CONFIRMATORY EVIDENCES. — SPECIAL PROVIDENCES AND DIVINE INSTRUMENTS. — CHRISTIAN CONSOLATION DERIVED FROM BELIEF IN ANGELIC MINISTRATIONS. — THE HOPE OF THE CHRISTIAN IN RELATION TO ANGELIC LIFE.

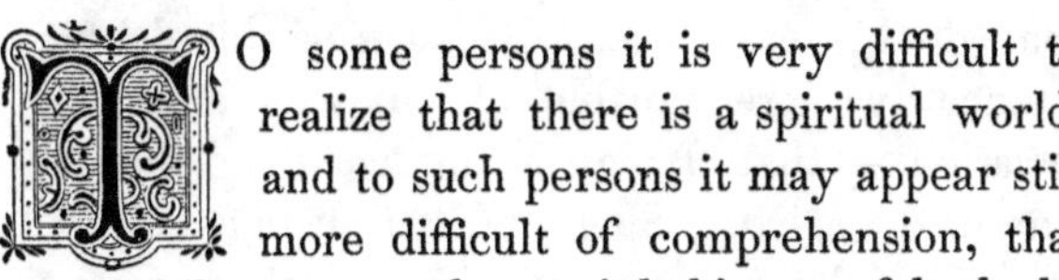

TO some persons it is very difficult to realize that there is a spiritual world, and to such persons it may appear still more difficult of comprehension, that men, while upon earth, are inhabitants of both the natural and spiritual worlds. Yet it requires only a small amount of consideration to perceive that this must be the fact. We are connected with the natural universe by our physical existence, and we are acquainted with its objects by the means of our senses; but we can think of ideas which the natural world does not present to us, and of which it offers us but dim mirrors and faint echoes. While still dwelling in time, we can meditate upon eternity; in the midst of the limitations of space, we can conceive of a state not subject to its restrictions. Our own consciousness manifests to us that there is something within us above nature. Revelation itself comes to us as a *super*-natural thing. The idea of God, the author of external nature, is possible to us; and the fact of this possibility proves us to be superior to external nature, — the sensual universe; — proves us, therefore, to be *supernatural.* Fettered by its temporary connection with the sensual world, by its union with the body, our consciousness in its *normal* condition is far more physical than spiritual; yet all have at times glimpses of something grander than a mere physical being. And these glimpses, however transient and faint they may be, are still evidences of our double existence. Because of this double existence, we are capable of enjoying a double association, — that of man in the flesh, and that of spirits in the spirit. Such spiritual beings may be no more visible to our physical senses than are the spirits of men in the flesh visible to our physical senses; yet in neither case is the invisibility of the spirit a proof of its non-existence, nor an evidence of its non-presence.

It appears, at least, remarkable, that in this age when men universally boast of *intellect*, its progress, its discoveries, its development, and its triumphs, that they should be inclined to doubt or ridicule the existence of spirit. The soul of man is man's spiritual constitution, and intellect is one of its sublime functions or powers. The very intellect that they boast is the refutation of their own denial of spirit. Enveloped in this transitory tabernacle of clay, we are spiritual beings with spiritual powers, of which the physical powers are only the instruments that enable us to do our work, and to render our purposes and thoughts visible by enacting them in this mundane sphere: but we are spiritual beings still, clothed on with a natural or physical investiture. Although it has unhappily become the fashion to despise such convictions as fanatical, there is nothing in them repugnant to the severest reason or the soundest philosophy. Indeed, the severest reason will only be the most satisfied that its intellectual faculties are the powers of a spiritual being possessing them, and hence be the most convinced of the existence of spirit. That we are spiritual beings is a fact which is patent to the consciousness of all, and it is only by a long and laborious process of reasoning that a few can convince themselves of the contrary; and, after all, the convictions they have thus acquired are terribly liable to be shaken by the moral earthquake of doubt.

In any case the testimony of the Word of God is irrefutable on this subject, and it unquestionably teaches us that we are spiritual beings surrounded by the inhabitants of the spiritual world. As such, we may have to do with angels as well as men, — both our fellow-creatures, the ones wholly resident in the world to which, as spirits, we belong; the others, like ourselves, heirs of immortality, who are for a time incorporated in the flesh. We cannot but feel, therefore, a lively, because personal, interest in all that concerns the angels, especially so far as regards their being our guardians, companions, and guides. The Bible furnishes us with many bright glimpses of such heavenly associations, illustrating the subject by examples, and confirming the fact by explicit statements.

Angels are certainly *intelligent* beings. We read of their singing songs, bearing messages to the prophets and other servants of God, performing important missions among men, sometimes of mercy, and at other times of wrath and destruction. These acts presuppose, and, indeed, necessitate, their possession of intelligence.

Angels are also *loving* beings, that is, not only susceptible of receiving, but of reciprocating, God's love for them, and also possessed of vast love and tenderness towards each other, and likewise towards mankind. The Psalmist asserts, "In his presence there is fulness of joy; at his right hand there are pleasures forevermore."[1] This proves the capacity of love possessed by the angels; for

[1] Ps. xvi. 11.

their joy in the presence of God is only the result of their love to God. The Lord declares, "There is joy in the presence of God among the angels over one sinner that repenteth."[1] This evinces how close must be the connection between heaven and earth, how constant must be the supervision of earth by the angels of heaven, how *individual*, indeed, must be that supervision; and not only individual as to each human being, but also as to every particular state and frame of mind in each individual; and it further proves how tender must be the love which angels bear to man. The depth of the interest they take in man is the evidence of their love for him.

Angels, further, are *active* beings. Proofs of the vast powers intrusted to or possessed by them abound in the Word of God. In the Passover, the instrument of Divine judgment was an angel. In the destruction of the hosts of Sennacherib, the instrument of the Lord was an angel. In the various desolations revealed in the Apocalypse, God accomplishes His purposes through the mediumship of angels, and employs them as the instruments of His designs. The Psalmist directly asserts their power. "Bless the Lord, ye his angels, *that excel in strength*, that do his commandments, hearkening unto the voice of his word."[2]

Not only do angels possess intelligence, affection, and activities, — which also form the spiritual na-

1 Luke xv. 10. 1 Ps. ciii. 20.

ture of all men, and, therefore, the angels may and, indeed, must be, regarded as spiritual men, — but the constant declaration and suggestion of the Bible is that they are likewise *human in form.* They are invariably described as *men.* In one particular case, when an angel appeared to Manoah and his wife, he seemed so to resemble a man that they knew not but that he was a man; and not till "the angel did wondrously, and ascended in the flame of the altar,"[1] did the parents of Samson know that he was an angel: "Then Manoah knew that he was an angel of the Lord." Not only in their appearances with special missions to individuals, but also when beheld by the Prophet Daniel and the Apostle John, in the forms that are their own in heaven, they are invariably described as men, more exquisitely beautiful than men on earth, radiant with glory, harmonizing with the loveliness and grandeur of their dwelling-place, but still MEN. It is impossible to conceive of them in any other shape than the human. Wings are a fancy which symbolism has depicted, as an emblem of their powers of movement and ascension; but even the idea of their possessing wings never had a serious lodgement in our conceptions of them.

> "Angels are men in lighter habit clad,
> And men are angels loaded for an hour."

From these four postulates as to the nature of angels, — their being intelligent, loving, and active

[1] Judg. xiii. 19, 20.

beings in the human form, — several important consequences result. As they are loving beings, loving not only God who is above them, but man who is their inferior, they must desire to benefit and serve man. As they are intelligent beings, they must know how most effectually to consummate their desire. As they are endowed with vast powers of action, powers superior to any that we can adequately conceive of, they must be able to accomplish what their love for man has prompted, and what their intelligence has shown them how to accomplish. Angels are therefore the servants of and ministers unto man. And from analogy also this conclusion seems inevitable. Men on earth who largely love their kind, desire the most ardently to serve their fellow-beings. The desire to serve is the measure by which their affection may be tested. When to their love they add great intelligence, the method and nature of the service which they can best render is seen by them ; their desire prompts, and their intelligence directs them. And when to their love and intelligence they can add vast powers of action, — whether it be from the high positions they occupy and the wide influence such positions enable them to command, or from the energy they possess, and the persevering endurance which such energy confers, or from the wealth intrusted to them, and the instrumentalities which such wealth bestows, — their desire to help, and their knowledge how to help efficiently, find expression in deeds of service and labors of use. So of the angels. We can only think of them as men immensely more loving, more intelligent, and more powerful than any man on earth, — yet glorified men who dwell above, and who are still laboring for the good and help of suffering man below.

But as they are human in form, as well as intensely human in their interest in man, so their operation upon man must be to some extent analogous to the operation of man upon his fellow-creatures. The mode by which they most constantly operate must therefore be by endeavoring to impress his will through his affections, his understanding through his thoughts. This does not require that the angels should be visible to man. We are often most influenced by our fellow-men when they are absent from our sight. The principles of knowledge they have taught us, and their maxims of wisdom which we remember, are often the most active within us when we have gone out from their presence. Memory forges the subtle chain by which we are bound to them. Their thoughts have become our thoughts, their affections our sentiments; and even though they be dead, they "rule us from their urns." Admit, as we must, that angelic beings possess interior means of impressing their thoughts on our minds, and their emotions on our hearts, and we can see at once that though invisible they can still influence us. If we are influenced by such beings at all, it must be through our human minds and hearts; while those who can thus influence us by affections and thoughts, must likewise be human too.

This, the argument from the nature of things, and from analogy, is abundantly supported by all that the Scriptures teach us on the subject. It was the faith of Abraham. When sending his steward to seek a wife for his son Isaac, he declares, "Jehovah, God of heaven, who took me from my father's house and sware unto me, saying, Unto thy seed will I give this land; he shall send *his angel* before thee, and thou shalt take a wife unto my son from thence."[1] This was also the consoling faith of Jacob. When he was blessing the sons of Joseph, he said, "*The angel which redeemed me from all evil*, bless the lads, and let my name be named on them, and the name of my fathers Abraham and Isaac."[2] It was the faith of Moses, and God himself teaches him to believe it. "*Behold I send an angel before thee*, to keep thee in the way, and to bring thee into the place which I have prepared. Beware of him, and obey his voice, provoke him not; for he will not pardon your transgressions: for my name is in him. But if thou shalt indeed obey his voice, and do all that I speak; then I will be an enemy of thine enemies, and an adversary unto thine adversaries. For mine angel shall go before thee, and bring thee unto the [land]."[3] Again, "And the Lord said unto Moses,

[1] Gen. xxiv. 7. [2] Gen. xlviii. 16. [3] Ex. xxiii. 20-23.

Whosoever hath sinned against me, him will I blot out of my book. Therefore go now, lead the people unto the place of which I have spoken unto thee: *behold, mine angel shall go before thee:* nevertheless, in the day when I visit, I will visit their sin upon them."[1] Again we read, "And *I will send an angel before thee;* and I will drive out the Canaanite, the Amorite, and the Hittite, and the Perizzite, the Hivite, and the Jebusite."[2] Joshua must also have cherished this faith, and could not help believing that the Lord had permitted him to behold such an angel, commissioned to aid Israel in their warfare. "And it came to pass, when Joshua was by Jericho, that he lifted up his eyes and looked, and, behold, there stood a man over against him with his sword drawn in his hand: and Joshua went unto him, and said unto him, Art thou for us, or for our adversaries? And he said, Nay; but as captain of the host of the Lord am I now come. And Joshua fell on his face to the earth, and did worship, and said unto him, What saith my lord to his servant? And the captain of the Lord's host said unto Joshua, Loose thy shoe from off thy foot; for the place whereon thou standest is holy. And Joshua did so."[3] The Israelites, in like manner, must have treasured this sublime faith; for these declarations were written for their instruction, and revered by them as the sacred oracles of God. Jehovah by his angels

[1] Ex. xxxii. 33, 34. [2] Ex. xxxiii. 2. [3] Josh. v. 13-15.

wrought their deliverance; and gratitude to Him and tenderness for them must have filled their souls. This was the message "sent from Kadesh unto the king of Edom, Thus saith thy brother Israel, Thou knowest all the travel that hath befallen us: how our fathers went down into Egypt, and we have dwelt in Egypt a long time; and the Egyptians vexed us, and our fathers: and when we cried unto the Lord, he heard our voice, and *sent an angel*, and hath brought us forth out of Egypt: and, behold, we are in Kadesh, a city in the uttermost of thy border."[1] Even to the heathen the Israelites were monuments of the providence of God, and of the ministry of angels. The supernatural incidents in their history are attributed to a machinery that is supernatural too, the instrumentality of angels, who are supernatural beings. "In all their afflictions he was afflicted, *and the angel of his presence* saved them."[2]

The cumulative force of these testimonies is irresistible as to the Israelites being the subjects of angelic assistance. But it may be properly urged that these were exceptional persons and that those were exceptional times. As the Lord had providential purposes which the Israelites were intended to fulfil, so He made use of extraordinary instruments for the realization of His designs: that we must not argue from the exception to the rule, from the individual to the universal: that it is

1 Num. xx. 14-16. 2 Isa. lxiii. 9.

therefore assuming too much to assert that because such was the method of Divine operation in respect to Israel, such also must be the method of Divine operation in regard to all mankind. The force of these objections we admit; and were the testimonies of angelic interposition in human affairs limited even to the strong instances already cited, we might admire the grandeur of the agencies employed in the case of the Israelites, but should not feel warranted in affirming them to be particular illustrations and open exhibitions of a general method. Fortunately for our argument and for our conviction, such testimonies stand not alone as referring to Israel exclusively. Although the number of the appearances of angels in Israelitish history affords the basis for a presumptive inference in favor of universal angelic guardianship and guidance of man, yet in such a matter we need more than a presumption, however probable it might seem. And the Bible furnishes us with explicit declarations in the matter.

Not only did angels openly appear, and thus manifest their agency to Abraham, Jacob, Joseph, Moses, Joshua, Manoah, Gideon, Elijah, Elisha, Isaiah, and the other prophets, but even to Balaam,[1] who appears to have known something of God, but yet to have been a bad man, and certainly not an Israelite. Yet this instance is open to the objection stated above, inasmuch as this appearance

[1] Num. xxii. 22-35.

of an angel had still to do with the Israelites, although indirectly. The cases described in the New Testament certainly supply additional illustrations of the open ministry of angels. Zecharias, Mary, Joseph, the shepherds, Peter, James and John, Paul, Philip, and the other disciples, were permitted to behold angelic beings. They appeared at the temptation, the transfiguration, the agony in the garden of Gethsemane, at the resurrection, and at the ascension of the Lord. The Apocalypse also is full of descriptions of such appearances. Still, in relation to the appearances of angels as recorded in the New Testament, it may be objected, that, as the Lord had then a special purpose to accomplish in the establishment of a new dispensation, in the revelation of himself in the flesh, and in the completion of His inspired Word, the peculiarity of these objects may have rendered necessary the adoption of peculiar instrumentalities, as special means for a special purpose; and that therefore it is again assuming too much to argue from the extraordinary to the ordinary, from the special to the universal. While this may be conceded, yet one general conclusion is evident, — that whenever God has had special designs to accomplish, angels have been His messengers and instruments. This affords us a glimpse, which is full of interest and significance, of the mode adopted by the Lord for the special operations of His Divine providence.

There is, however, a more correct method of stating the proposition above indicated, which is indeed the only logical conclusion from the facts. The corollary as stated above indicates a presumption that only on special and extraordinary occasions do angels minister unto man, which presumption we believe to be false. The more exact conclusion is, that only on special and extraordinary occasions have men been *made conscious* of angelic ministrations, by being *permitted to see* the angels. The specialty of the cases did not consist in the *ministration* itself, but in the *openness* of the ministration. At other times invisible, the angels on these particular occasions were suffered to appear visibly before the subjects of their ministry; and such *visible* appearances were rendered possible by the opening of the spiritual sight of the beholders. There is an important difference in the results of the two methods of stating the proposition. In the one case the *ministration* is extraordinary, and in the other it is only the *openness* of the ministration.

It is surely more conducive to the dignity of God, and better exemplifies the invariableness of His operation, and the impartiality of His love for man, as well as more accordant with the argument from the nature of angels, to believe that angelic ministrations are constant and universal, and that the extraordinary nature of the Scriptural narratives of such ministrations consist in their openness and visibility, than it is to believe that angelic ministrations are unusual, extraordinary, and special, — a marvellous derangement of the economy of existence, a phenomenon unprecedented previously, and without parallel afterwards. This proposition, which is so consonant with reason, is also sufficiently intimated in the Bible. The Psalmist declares, "The angel of the Lord encampeth round about them that fear him, and delivereth them."[1] This statement is as universal, at least as far as those who "fear the Lord" are universal. Wherever such may be found, they are, by this declaration, justified in believing that the angel of the Lord is near them, to be to them, as to Israel of old, "the angel of their deliverance." The Psalmist again affirms, "Because thou hast made the Lord, who is my refuge, even the Most High thy habitation, there shall no evil befall thee, neither shall any plague come nigh thy dwelling. For he shall give his angels charge over thee, to keep thee in all thy ways."[2] In view of Matthew iv., and the fact of this passage being partly cited in the temptation of Jesus, we must conclude that this promise bears *primary* reference to the Lord Jesus Christ; yet is its meaning to be no more limited to Him, than is the application of the other declarations of the Psalms. We regard it rather as the assertion of a universal fact, in which the Divine humanity of the Lord, the Son Jesus, was included, as well as every other being who makes "the Lord his habi-

[1] Ps. xxxiv. 7. [2] Ps. xci. 11.

tation." It refers to Jesus *primarily*, because Jesus is the pattern of His disciples, the glorification of the human nature assumed by Him being the exact pattern or type of the regeneration of His people. "The children of God" are "heirs of God, and *joint-heirs* with Christ," and "if so be we suffer with him, we may be also glorified together."[1] While, then, they are "heirs according to the promise,"[2] and therefore *heirs of all the promises* made by God, this blessing of angelic ministration is theirs by right of inheritance; and their faith falls short of their birthright if they do not believe and cherish it.

The perception of these truths vastly widens the sphere of angelic ministrations, showing them to extend, at least, to all Christians. But the Lord Jesus has affirmed them to be more universal still. He declares of all children, "Take heed that ye despise not one of these little ones; for I say unto you, That in heaven their angels do always behold the face of my Father who is in heaven."[3] What is the meaning of this statement, if it be not that every child is under the guardianship of an angel, and that these angels are of the highest and holiest order, "always beholding the face of God in heaven"? Mothers, at least, may know, and joy in the knowledge, that the dear objects of their tender love are beloved by higher and better beings than themselves; that not only

[1] Rom. viii. 17. [2] Gal. iii. 29. [3] Matt. xviii. 10.

is God's merciful providence continually over their darlings, but that, as instruments of that providence, there are angels who love them with more than human devotion, who watch over them with more than human vigilance, and who may guard them with an intelligence which likewise is more than human. These helpless babes are eternal beings, born into the spiritual as well as into the natural world, surrounded by the inhabitants of both worlds, to be subject to the influences which both worlds can bring to bear upon them: and the results of all these various influences and agencies will be eliminated and fixed in the final state the infants make their own. It is a consideration which enhances the mystery of life, even while it elucidates it; which exalts the majesty of existence, and enlarges the place which every human creature fills in the vast economy of being. Human relations lay hold on universal existence, and the dwellers in both the spiritual and natural places are gainers by every child that is born.

Children are certainly, therefore, under the especial protection and guidance of angels; but the question forces itself upon our minds, When do the angels forsake the child? Is it in the struggles and commencing temptations of youth? in the deeper trials and severe mental conflicts of young manhood? in the fiercer strifes and more desperate encounters of maturity? or is it in the decrepitude and second infancy of old age? Having been the subject of angelic care, and the object of angelic tenderness for so long, do the angels weary of their mission, or does man become incapable of receiving their aid? The changes which take place in man's state and spiritual condition may affect the order and class of angels attending him, and this may be the meaning of the limitation expressed in the Lord's words, "*Their* angels do always behold the face of my Father"; but as He separates himself from these, may not *others* continue their loving cares and their unfailing attendance? Separated by a change in his necessities — the result of his mental and moral development — from this order of angels, man still continues to be the heir to the promises of "angels of the Lord having charge over him, to keep him in all his ways." The question, When are they present? is better put, When are they wholly absent? The number of such angels is countless, and Paul asserts a great principle in the form of a question, "Are they not ALL ministering spirits, sent forth to minister unto them who shall be heirs of salvation?"[1]

There is, further, afforded in the Bible a glimpse of a very remarkable fact. The Prophet Daniel has been praying "and mourning three full weeks; he ate no pleasant bread, neither came flesh nor wine into his mouth, neither did he anoint himself at all till three whole weeks were fulfilled. And

[1] Heb. i. 14.

in the four-and-twentieth day of the first month, as he was by the side of the great river, which is Hiddekel, he lifted up his eyes and beheld a certain man clothed in linen." This man was exceedingly glorious. He was seen by Daniel alone, and the men who were with him fled away to hide themselves. This man was an angel of God, who touched Daniel, and said, "O Daniel, a man greaty beloved, understand the words that I speak unto thee, and stand upright: for unto thee am I now sent. . . . . Fear not, Daniel: for from the first day thou didst set thy heart to understand, and to chasten thyself before thy God, thy words were heard, and I am come for thy words. But the prince of the kingdom of Persia withstood me one-and-twenty days: but, lo, Michael, one of the chief princes, came to help me; and I remained there with the kings of Persia. Now am I come to make thee understand what shall befall thy people in the latter days."[1] After sundry other incidents, the angel continues, "Knowest thou wherefore I come unto thee? and now will I return to fight with the prince of Persia: and when I am gone forth, lo, the prince of Grecia shall come. But I will show thee that which is noted in the scripture of truth: and there is none that holdeth with me in these things, but Michael your prince."[2] This remarkable passage indicates several things: first, that angels are employed to answer prayer;

[1] Dan. x. 2 - 14. [2] verses 20, 21.

secondly, that in the case of the prophet this ministration was not only *real*, but *also visible ;* thirdly, that the angels have other employments which may prevent their immediate performance of any one duty assigned to them ; fourthly, that not only did Daniel, but that also others do, enjoy such angelic ministrations, although the angels may remain to these other persons invisible ; fifthly, that the nature of angelic employment may include even opposition and conflict with superhuman beings of a totally different character, who seek to impede or frustrate the merciful intentions of God ; — such beings here alluded to as "the prince of Persia, and the prince of [Javan or] Grecia"; sixthly, that these angels are associated together, and mutually assist each other in the performance of the missions committed to them ; seventhly, that such a one was Michael, here called "a prince," and in Jude called "an archangel" (Jude 9), and again, in Dan. xii. 1, described as "Michael the great prince who standeth up for the children of thy people."

"Most commentators suppose this passage to contain an intimation of the existence of tutelary angels, good and bad ; and that the 'prince of Persia' and the 'prince of Grecia' represent superhuman beings acting as patrons of those nations, and devoted to their interests."[1]

The general conclusions which in this place we

[1] The Tract Society's Annotated Bible, Comment on Dan. x.

seek to enforce from this passage are, that all men are attended by angels; — that such attendance is according to the state and necessities of the individual so attended, — in fine, that angelic ministrations are not merely special and extraordinary, but ordinary and universal. The cases of such ministrations described in Holy Writ are only illustrations of a universal fact, and the specialty of those cases consists, not in the special and exceptional permission of the ministration, but in the special and peculiar *character* of the messages they communicated, or in the missions they performed. This glorious picture has, however, an obverse side. The Bible intimates the ministration or attendance of malevolent spirits, whose feeling toward those whom they attend is the attraction of hatred, and whose effort is for their destruction. This is indicated in the passage cited above from Daniel, where the princes of Persia and Grecia have to be combated against by the angel. It is further shown by the Psalmist: "He cast upon them the fierceness of his anger, wrath, and indignation, and trouble, *by sending evil angels among them.*"[1] It is illustrated in the Gospel histories, by those unfortunates who "were possessed by devils." It is confirmed by the parable of the Saviour, of the man out of whom "the unclean spirit hath gone, who walketh through dry places, seeking rest and finding none, who goeth and taketh with him-

[1] Ps. lxxviii. 49.

self seven other spirits, more wicked than himself, and they enter in and dwell there: and the last state of that man is worse than the first."[1]

A strong argument in confirmation of this view of superhuman ministration might be adduced from the common assent of mankind, from the reasonings of philosophers, and the intuitions of ancient and modern poetry; but as these glimpses of the spiritual world are designed to be drawn from the Bible revelation, we forbear from citing them. The individual experiences of Christian believers furnish us also with perhaps a more pertinent source of illustrative information. Whence come strong impulses, prophetic dreams, verified presentiments of danger, singular deliverances? Does it not seem reasonable to attribute some of them to impressions produced on the minds of their subjects by spiritual agents? Does not this comprehensive conception further enable us to understand what may be the secret of such men's lives as William Huntingdon, the author of the "Bank of Faith," as Müller, the extraordinary philanthropist of Bristol, as Oberlin, the heroic pastor of Ban de la Roche, as Jung Stilling, as Martin Luther, particularly in respect of his remarkable communions with spiritual beings, as well as a host of others whom we might name? To deny the statements of such men is only learned trifling. Far apart from each other, they affirm similar facts; facts, too, which, had they

[1] Luke xi. 24 - 26.

listened to self-interest or prejudice, they would have concealed; and facts which, coming to us so sufficiently substantiated, compel our credence and demand explanation. Unless we admit such spiritual ministrations, it has been found impossible to offer any explanation at all.

The interposition of Divine providence by the mediumship of loving, intelligent, mighty beings, spiritual men in the spiritual world, does appear to be of easier apprehension than interference without such agencies; while also its nature involves nothing unworthy of God, and nothing contradictory to the declarations of the Bible. A man may be to his fellows an instrument of help and comfort, of succor and rescue, and we call his intervention a manifestation of providence; surely, then, if similar interventions are effected through the instrumentality of angels, they also will deserve to be regarded as a manifestation of providence. The fact of the Lord's employing men as His instruments does not derogate from His dignity; and the further fact of His making angels His ministers or agents cannot detract from His glory, nor diminish our gratitude and praise. Whatever other vast and untraceable modes of operation the Divine providence adopts, more potent and more immediate than even angelic agencies, yet we must conclude that among His modes of operation the agency of angels and spirits occupies a prominent and important place. We seek not to limit the modes of Divine operation, which may be as infinite in their variety as He is infinite in His love and wisdom, or, at least, as varied in their forms as the necessities and capacities of His creatures are diversified in their character; but we do seek to explore what it hath pleased Him to reveal, and not to narrow by prejudice or ignorance our knowledge of the full range of His Divine operation through the agency of spiritual beings.

We may be sure of this, that in the sight of God and in the laws of His Divine government, the natural and the spiritual worlds are as *one.* They are inextricably interlinked and indissolubly interblended, pervaded by an intelligence variously received, yet received by all alike from one common source,—Himself. These two worlds are neither remote nor inert, neither distant from nor inactive towards each other. There is a blessed and continual "communion of saints" consisting, on the one side, of "the spirits of just men made perfect," who have "entered into their rest," and who dwell in "eternal habitations, houses not made with hands," and, on the other, of those who are still fighting the fight and toiling in the mundane pilgrimage of faith. The militant church below and the triumphant church above, in the sight of God compose but one church; however separated they may be in the spheres of their existence, they are yet united by the bonds of fellowship and the cords of love. Those above are with us here below, and so intimate and so sympathizing are they with our real conditions, that the contrition of the penitent, when full of godly sorrow, diffuses a richer joy among the angels, and even enhances the felicity of heaven. "There is joy in heaven over one sinner that repenteth." The poet has only thrilled a deep and true-sounding chord, and caught the gleam of a glorious fact, in the conception that the tear-drop of penitence finds favor and acceptance in heaven.

We need not say how strengthening to our faith in God, how comforting in our states of affliction, how confirmatory of our hopes of the future, are such convictions. Life is a grander thing than we had before thought it; for it is provided with a nobler promise, and is supplied with an object that is more august. Angels are men perfected, and we are angels in embryo, who may confidently look forward in hope, knowing the dignity of our destiny and the mercy of the Lord. Those angel-brothers of ours are only the illustrations of what every Christian may aspire to be, — spiritual men, gifted with deeper love, endowed with clearer intelligence, recipients of grander powers, having intrusted to them higher missions, nobler duties, sublimer enterprises; — all creation the fields of their labor, all humanity the objects of their love, human salvation the purpose of their existence, and the will of their and our Divine Father their source of joy and their abiding glory.

# III.

## HEAVENLY SCENERY.

"And he showed me a pure river of water of life, clear as crystal, proceeding out of the throne of God and of the Lamb. In the midst of the street of it, and on either side of the river, was there the tree of life, which bare twelve manner of fruits, and yielded her fruit every month." — REV. xxii. 1, 2.

THE ORDINARILY ENTERTAINED CONCEPTIONS OF HEAVEN. — TRUE SUBLIMITY. — THE MAINTENANCE OF UNITY IN VARIETY THE LAW OF DIVINE OPERATION. — THIS LAW OPERATIVE IN HEAVEN. — THE ARGUMENT FROM MAN'S NATURE. — ÆSTHETICAL LOVES, AND THE WANTS THEY INSPIRE. — MAN TAKES THEM WITH HIM INTO THE OTHER LIFE. — SCRIPTURE CONFIRMATIONS. — MUSIC IN HEAVEN, AND ITS CONSEQUENCES BY ANALOGY. — DESCRIPTIONS OF HEAVEN IN THE BIBLE. — THE PRINCIPLE OF HARMONY THE PREDOMINATING LAW IN HEAVEN. — THE LAW OF CORRESPONDENCE BETWEEN THE OBJECTIVE WORLD AND SUBJECTIVE STATES OF THE SOUL. — THE BEAUTIFUL IN HEAVEN. — THE REDEEMED IN HEAVEN REGENERATED AND SANCTIFIED, NOT TRANSFORMED. — THE VARIETIES OF INDIVIDUAL GENIUS RETAINED IN HEAVEN. — HEAVEN HUMAN, AND FITTED FOR MAN AS MAN IS FITTED FOR HEAVEN. — THE OBJECTION, HEAVEN ONLY AN IDEALLY BEAUTIFUL EARTH, CONSIDERED. — HEAVEN, "THE GARDEN OF GOD."

MOST vague and unsatisfactory have been the conceptions entertained by Christians as to the nature of heavenly scenery and heavenly habitations. To judge from the expressions of some writers, it would appear as though they imagined heaven to be a vast plain, or an immense temple, where were grouped harping multitudes, "loud in their praise, unceasing in their hymn." Many have thus depicted heaven, even while declaring that they would forbear the attempt to idealize any picture of what it is. If, however, they speak of heaven at all, they are compelled to contradict themselves; for it is inevitable that we must form some conception of anything of which we speak. Notwithstanding the reverential awe with which every one must approach the subject, and despite any disclaimer we may make, the very process of thought necessitates some idea, and the grander that idea, the more satisfactory has it been. Whatever some may seem to conjecture, *vagueness* does not really enhance the sublimity of heaven; its attractiveness does not increase with its incomprehensibility. The truly sublime must ever possess some characteristics which lie beyond the competent grasp of the mind, although not altogether beyond the range of imagination. But unless we can see some characteristics, and unless those characteristics which we do see are worthy to be associated with those other and higher characteristics which lie beyond sight, and which, therefore, can only be imagined, there is neither sublimity nor anything. Partial concealment with partial revelation is the great secret of sublimity. The ideas of vastness and grandeur necessarily enter into our conception of the sublime. But these are only terms of relation, and imply comparison. The standard of comparison which we are compelled to employ is ourselves. But yet, while the far-off may be indistinct, we can only believe in that indistinct distance by comparing it with the more distinct objects that fill the foreground.

Heaven is promised to the faithful as an object of hope, and is designed to act as an inducement. While it is sufficiently revealed to show that its existence is a certainty, it is sufficiently concealed to require diligent consideration and research to learn something of its nature. More even than this, it is so concealed, that what we can learn forms but the very smallest part of heaven: the rest is yet inconceivable. The hope that it promises and the inducements that it presents, however, can only become stronger as our apprehension of its nature becomes clearer. It is not presumptuous, consequently, to endeavor to learn something of the character of heavenly scenery. We can, at most, only learn what is possible to be learned, and what the Lord, therefore, designed us to know.

So far as we can learn the plan of Divine operation in the material universe, it seems to be the preservation of an unchangeable UNITY in a constantly changing and endless VARIETY. Creation, though manifold, is yet one. The classifications of natural objects into kingdoms, groups, orders, divisions, genus, and species, is the effort to chronicle both these great features. Both the Unity of God and His Infinitude find here their exemplifications. Such a variety in unity on earth only enhances our reverence for God. Both are necessary to enable us to form anything like an approximate perception of His Divine Perfection. Were earth an unvaried and monotonous plain, were the firmament a dark expanse, unbrightened by a star, were animated nature only of one order, and vegetation of only one species, our perception of God's marvellous wisdom and power would be dwarfed and stultified. Inadequate as it is at best, it would then shrink into a still sadder inadequacy: the universe would not so well manifest its Creator, and man would know less of God. But if earth by its variety exhibits so much of the Divine nature, so far as the workmanship exhibits the workman, then heaven must exhibit such a various proof of God still more markedly; that is, heaven must be a more illustrative portraiture of God. His Divine Unity must be evinced in the unity that prevails there, and His Divine Infinitude in the immense variety which must prevail there too.

We have before seen that there is variety in the heavens themselves; that there are distinctions between the angels, according to their capacities of receiving the Divine gifts, or of exercising their derived powers; and we may further see that such a variety must and does extend to the places of their abode, and the scenery that surrounds them.

We have, first, the argument from man's nature. God has implanted in man the love of the picturesque, of the beautiful, of the sublime. These loves are not of mere abstract qualities, — not of beauty, or sublimity, as *abstract* or *general ideas*, but of objects that are beautiful or sublime. Loving such things, we desire to behold objects that may minister to the gratification of those loves. Those persons are the most fully human, that is, they are most fully endowed with the noblest human qualities, in whom such loves are the most largely developed. There is a double evidence of Divine goodness in the bestowal of such tastes: first, that man may derive enjoyment from the works of His hands; and, secondly, that in perceiving the beauty and sublimity of His Divine productions, they may conceive of the beauty and sublimity of the nature and character of their Divine Producer. They show the adaptability of nature to the constitution of man, and, further, the sufficiency of nature to be the mirror in which man may dimly see God.

These æsthetical loves certainly belong to the spiritual side of man's being, and, consequently, it is only just to conclude that man will take them with him into the other life. It would be contrary to all that we are obliged to conceive of the nature of angels, to suppose that they are incapable of experiencing delight from such æsthetic gratifications. More lovely than man, they must share more largely than he in the love of the beautiful. Sublimer existences, their power of perceiving and appreciating the sublime must be far superior to what man possesses. But the love will engender the desire; the appreciation of the beautiful will instigate the craving to behold the beautiful. In permitting the desire to be felt, God has manifested His purpose of ministering to that desire by the supply of the object desired. A holy want is the prophet and precursor of its own fulfilment. To admit that such a love, such an appreciation, such a desire can exist in heaven, is, therefore, virtually to admit that in heaven there must exist the beautiful, the picturesque, and the sublime in scenery. The angels themselves are surpassingly lovely. God gratifies the love of the beautiful implanted in the angels by making the angels fair and lovely to look upon; and does not this suggest that all that surrounds them must be beautiful also? Ministering to this æsthetic taste in relation to the features and persons of each other, is it not reasonable to conclude that God further ministers to this want in the scenery by which they are environed?

The Psalmist declares that "in heaven there is fulness of joy"; not only because the joy will be full as to the gratification of some *one particular* disposition of the soul; but because heaven is full of objects that can delight *every* pure and holy desire. The fulness there must supply man's full and complete nature, and make of every separate faculty implanted within him a various recipient of the Divine mercies. No want that is pure and holy can there remain unsatisfied; and as his æsthetic wants are pure in themselves and holy in their influences, and as they will remain to man after the transit from time into eternity, we must conclude that heaven will present "of its fulness" to their ample gratification; and that, therefore, beautiful scenery must exist there.

To this eminently reasonable view the Word of God adds strong confirmation.

The Apostle asserts that "eye hath not seen, ear hath not heard, neither have entered into the heart of man, the things which God hath prepared for them that love him."[1] This declaration is often applied to the things of heaven, though the context will show that the Apostle understood the words as rather referring to the advent of the Lord into the flesh. But even as commonly applied, the passage only declares that the things prepared are *above* human conception, not that they are *contrary* to what we can conceive of heaven. They may infinitely surpass the highest idea in *degree*, and present *kinds* of enjoyment which at present are altogether unknown to us; yet what we know of man's mental constitution, and what we can learn from the Bible of the mental constitution of angels, serve to indicate to some extent the nature of some of the heavenly things prepared for us.

[1] 1 Cor. ii. 9.

One of the most frequently repeated details of heavenly enjoyment is *music.* And what we know of the marvellous power and exquisite beauty of music eminently fits it to be regarded as suitable for heaven. The idea of "quiring symphonies of young-eyed cherubim" is so accordant with man's noblest nature as to be altogether in harmony with his conception of heaven. It is also an indication of a great principle. We can appreciate and love music here. Even though limited by the restrictions which time and matter impose upon us, yet this love of music is the inception of a heavenly taste, and our enjoyment of it is a foretaste of a heavenly enjoyment. The love of music, however, is but one of a wide group of loves. Music is the beautiful in sound, as scenery is the beautiful to sight; and if the love of the beautiful as *heard,* is to be delighted in heaven, why not the love of the beautiful as *beheld?* The music of earth to the harmony of heaven may be as the glimmer of moonlight to the glory of the sunshine, yet though different in *degree,* it is still similar in *kind.* Our knowledge of the *kind* of delight afforded by our experience of earthly music may enable us to form a conception of the higher *degree.* The conception may be inadequate, and yet, so far as it can reach, it may be an approximation to the reality. And so in like manner with the beautiful in scenery. It would be folly to attempt to describe the details of heavenly scenery, but the general idea stands sufficiently out to justify belief. The most glorious bursts of harmony that ever thrilled and quivered through the brain of Handel, the pealing triumphs of the "Hallelujah Chorus," the glowing snatches of Mozart, the gorgeous sonatas of Beethoven, the almost speaking melodies of Mendelssohn, and all the exquisite conceptions of the most gifted masters, may be only faint and far-off echoes to the grander performances above; yet as echoes they bring down something of heavenly music to the conceptions of men on earth, and make us yearn and bend before the thought, "If these be *echoes*, what must the realities be!" So again with heavenly scenery. If all on earth be only the shadows of the real in heaven, yet as shadows they may afford us a foreglimpse of the reality; and what must those realities be!

To the same general conclusions tend all the Bible visions of heaven, and the descriptions therein given to us. The inhabitants of heaven are ever represented as possessing *senses*, and senses imply objects of sense. Eyes imply things to be seen, as sounds to be heard presuppose the sense of hearing. Hence the prophets have been permitted to behold some of the objects of sight there. Take only the Book of Revelation. There are mentioned cities, the splendor of which dazzles the imagination; mountains varying in loftiness, and with mountains the idea of valleys is inevitably associated; rivers flowing on under a glory excelling the sunshine, and rippling out music as their waves dance along; trees with leaves and fruits more lovely to view, and more delicious to the taste, than the fabled apples of the Hesperides; waving palms, and temples transcending in magnificence all the most gorgeous fanes of earthly history, — the solemn colonnades of Egypt, the golden pomp of Jerusalem, the sombre vastness of India, the palatial splendor of Nineveh, the severe symmetry of Greece, the luxurious tinsel of Moresco, or those almost miracles in stone, wherein the Goths imitated the interlacing branches of their own forest trees. The Lord himself spoke of *mansions* in heaven.

"There everlasting spring abides,
  And never-fading flowers.
Death, like a narrow sea, divides
  That heavenly land from ours.

"Sweet fields, beyond the swelling flood,
  Stand dressed in living green;
So to the Jews their Canaan stood,
  While Jordan rolled between."

Scripture abundantly warrants the comparison adopted by the poet, that Canaan may be regarded as, to some extent, a symbol of heavenly scenery. Surpassing in beauty, in verdure, in spontaneous fruitfulness all other lands, — a garden-land that flung back the dewy freshness of the air and the sweet radiance of the skies, in delicious and lovely flowers, Canaan was a sort of second Eden, which is also most impressively styled "the garden of

God." The Prophet Ezekiel also beheld there hills, and mountains, and valleys, and rivers, and fountains, the holy city, and the temple of God. The Prophet Zechariah beheld olive-branches, and rivers, and lakes, and seas, and mountains, and groves. All these visions assert and justify the confidence that in heaven there are "fields forever fresh, and groves forever green." The great predominating feature of heavenly scenery must be *harmony* with the states of the angels. Because they are lovely from goodness, everything about them must be beautiful; because they are bright from wisdom, everything about them must be bright; because they are various among themselves, as being different from each other, so must there exist a variety equally diversified in the surrounding scenery; and because their individual life cannot be a wearisome monotony, because they must pass through such mental changes of state as are represented in the Scriptural expressions, morning, noon, and evening, therefore the scenery about any one of them must be susceptible of various changes.

The only possible *law*, or universal principle, which can obtain in heaven, whether it be in relation to heavenly scenery or the garments of the angels, is *subjective* in its nature. On earth, the fixity of matter presents the same external landscape to the beholders, however diverse in character, or however varying in state. We are conquered by the changeless objectivity of the natural plane; we are slaves to things external to ourselves. But in the things of the mind, our mental scenery is in harmony with, is indeed the outbirth and outgrowth of, our mental states. In heaven, this harmony is universal, and is the only law. Nearness and remoteness, sequence and order, are there spiritual states rendered into visible facts. The angels are as objectively near to each other as they are subjectively near; that is, they are *near* to, or *remote* from, each other in a double sense. Their spiritual nearness, or similarity, produces nearness of their spirits; their spiritual remoteness, or difference, produces remoteness of their spirits. Those who love God most are *nearest* to God, and the objective fact is only the manifestation, the consequence of the subjective state. *Here*, time and space are fixed facts, often strangely militating against subjective states of mind. Both time and space separate the lover from the beloved, the desire from its realization, the thinker from the subject of thought, and the result is restlessness, weariness, and pain. *There*, to wish is to have, to think of is to behold, to love is to be, and in the full consummation of the desire and the thought, joy unceasing and peace untroubled flow in upon the soul. Tears are wiped away in the extinction of sorrow, sighing is abolished in the realization of the wishes, peace reigns because the struggle is over, and joy is full because every affection that can be *there* cherished is the herald of its own gratification.

All the objects outwardly beheld in heaven are only the illustrations and manifestations of the actual inward state of the beholder. This, however, may not be fully understood without a previous comprehension of the fact that there exists a *correspondence* between all objects of sight and the affections and thoughts of the soul; so that the one is the complete and efficient symbol of the others. Even here on earth, the spiritual and natural planes are co-related. Man is the meeting-place, the *common ground* of both. He is at once both a *microcosm* and a *micro-ouranos*, a miniature of the world and also of heaven. He is at once both a spiritual and a natural being; the objects of sense come to his consciousness through the gates of his senses; and the affections and thoughts which belong to him as a spiritual being come to his consciousness through the spiritual avenues of his will and understanding. There is a harmony between them,—not only of suggestion, but further of correspondence. Objects of sense are the effigies, the symbols of affections and thoughts; types and antitypes, mutually representative of each other. All creation is a picture-language, expressive, firstly, of the affections and thoughts of the Divine mind, and also of such affections and thoughts as human minds may receive from the Divine fountain of all thought and affection. Because they represent the Divine, they must represent human thoughts and affections; for man is the finite miniature of the Infinite. Because the objects of sense are thus essentially representative, they can be, as they have been, used as the elements of picture-languages, as hieroglyphs. Were this the proper place, it might be satisfactorily shown that the Bible abundantly confirms and exemplifies such a correspondence of natural things to things spiritual. The general law is certain; and from this general law, controlled by its principle, and exhibiting its operation, proceed all the particulars of beauty and brightness in heaven, and all the varieties of darkness and horror in hell. They are correspondent to the diversity of states in the angels or the demons. Hence we may conclude that the revelations given in the Bible, of there being mountains and valleys, gardens and groves, rivers and lakes, forests and fields, gorgeous temples and resplendent mansions, and magnificent cities in heaven, are revelations of facts, — facts objectively visible to the dwellers in the everlasting habitations, "houses not made with hands."

The fine arts afford us only the adumbrations of heavenly things; *here* earthly, perishing, diminished, and dwarfed; *there* in all their godlike beauty, permanence, and grandeur. Are we lovers of the beautiful as fixed in the human face? Faces transcending all earthly conceptions of loveliness shall meet us *there*. Are we lovers of the beautiful as illustrated in the human form? Forms surpassing the most exquisite and the most majestic conceptions of Phidias, of Michael Angelo, or Raphael may *there* be seen. Are we lovers of the beautiful as exhibited in landscapes? Pictures to which the gorgeous dreams of Turner, or the mellowed sweetness of Claude Lorraine's conceptions were only faint shadows, shall *there* be beheld. The beauty of earth, if it is possible to remember it in heaven, shall seem only dim glimpses of a higher loveliness, caught by a few choice spirits, and copied in stone or on canvas by facile hands. Are we lovers of the beautiful as expressed in sound? Music as superior to the best below as heaven is higher than the earth, shall melt and peal among the "everlasting hills," and the ravished listeners shall with it drink in ecstasy. Are we lovers of the sublime in science? Truths of more than mortal range shall shine pellucid in heaven's spiritual light, and the soaring soul may ascend the starry stairway that leads up to the grander comprehension of God, the more adequate perception of His works, the deeper knowledge of His nature. Are we lovers of the sublime in eloquence? Angels' tongues shall pour forth the living streams of superhuman poetry, and the thirsty mind and hungry heart feed at the banquet of love and light. Man's noblest gifts are the incipient manifestations of a nature to be fully developed in heaven, and man's best wants are only the preparatives to the blissful realizations that await him there. God has portrayed the constitution of the heavenly man in the purest and noblest elements of our human nature, and written the secret of human destiny in the deep promptings of human hopes.

Heaven is not to be so utter a transformation of human character as shall obliterate all that is human from it, not the creation of an altogether new type and genus of being. *That* were to render unnecessary and useless the preparation which our earth-life was designed to afford; to destroy the connection between man on earth and the same man made heavenly; to abolish the indentity of the individual, the continued existence of the being. The truer thought is expressed in the phrase, "Man *made heavenly*," that is, the purification and sanctification of the individual. These processes exalt the character, not obliterate it; purify and sanctify the soul with all its individual aptitudes, and its idiosyncratic tastes. These latter adapt it to be useful in a way and for a purpose to which none other is so fit. They indicate and constitute the man's mission among men, and his angelic mission among the angels.

> "No compound of this earthly ball
> Is like another, all in all."

The variety which such individualities produce on earth only renders human society the more complete, and the variety of such individualities in heaven shall only render the angelic communion more full and perfect too. Heaven must be regarded as a state of *development* rather than of transformation. Individuality must survive in the preservation of identity, as identity must continue for the perpetuation of the man's existence. Individuality surviving, regeneration, then, can only be such a process as shall *make heavenly* all those various human characteristics which were in the beginning divinely implanted for the wisest of purposes. The redeemed ones shall be *men* with all the variety of powers, aptitudes, tastes, idiosyncrasies, and faculties which they possessed on earth, but in heaven to be devoted to holiness and consecrated to God, — upon the very "bells of the horses, HOLINESS TO THE LORD."[1]

Thus may mankind be relieved from the paralyzing fear that in heaven there is no room for human genius to expand, no range for the investigations of the scientific, no sphere for the meditations of the philosopher, no field for the delectation of art-lovers; but that all shall be reduced to a sombre uniformity of singers and harpists, and life to become a weary monotone. This last and commonly received idea, if not quite the *Nic Ban* of the Bhuddists, sufficiently resembles it to absorb all the marked lines and gradations of character and individuality; and from such a vision of heaven the mass of human strugglers intuitively recoil. Heaven is far more *human* than this; better adapted to seize hold on human thoughts and affections, because better adapted to human minds

[1] Zech. xiv. 20.

and hearts. Heaven is not so different from earth, but that holy men and women may already, even while here, catch a foregleam of its brightness, and receive the inchoation of its beauty and peace into their souls; and this, instead of obliterating their tastes, only purifies them; instead of absorbing their powers, sanctifies them; and instead of transforming them into a new genus and order of existences, renders their individualities more distinct than ever: distinct for the performance of spiritual uses, and defined by the devotion of every power or faculty to the worship and service of God. Regeneration defines human faculties, because it teaches men to discover them, in order that they may dedicate them; and to dedicate their faculties requires that they should exert them; and to exert their faculties only renders them more distinctly marked and more prominently developed. The good seed springs up within them, "in some thirty-fold, in some sixty-fold, and in some a hundred-fold"; but the richer they become in the gifts of the Lord's increase, the more mighty they become for manifold *uses;* and the manifold *uses* they can accomplish only establish within them some peculiar quality, some individual excellence, some especial grace possessed by no other soul. All that can minister to their development, and all that can make that development a never-failing joy to themselves, as well as an instrument of God to enhance the joy of all others, abounds in heaven. The variety of the angels has a corresponding variety in the scenery that surrounds them. The former adds an endless diversity of grace, of *use*, and of joy to the sum of happiness experienced in heaven as a *state;* and the latter variety adds a diversity equally endless to the beauty and sublimity of heaven as a place. Both are equally adapted to man's highest wants, and conformable to man's noblest conceptions; our earthly life of preparation can fit man for such a heaven, and the revelation of such a heaven is sufficient to prove its fitness for man. It furnishes an incentive to the cultivation of all that is pure and good in our nature, because it promises to that nature a development that shall be holy, and to that cultivation a success that shall never pass away.

We are aware it may be objected to these views, that they render heaven something like an ideally beautiful earth. The charge is admitted. It has grown by far too fashionable among certain classes to decry and declaim against the earth. To hear them, one would be led to the supposition that this beautiful world was an abomination in the sight of God and His angels; that loveliness had forsaken its vegetation, sublimity its scenery, freshness its meadows; and that an irradiant sun gloomily scowled on a panorama of desolation. There are deformities and disfigurements enough in the world; but these are the results of moral evil, and they are chiefly manifested in man. So long as distant ridges can melt away into the blue mists that surround them, so long as placid lakes can double the fleecy clouds that float over them, so long as brooks can flash in the sunshine from out of dusky bowers and green leaves, so long as the uncultivated prairies, and pampas, and savannahs shall continue carpeted with fresh grass and bright flowers, so long as lordly trees nod their proud heads to the kisses of the evening zephyrs, so long as the maiden spring adorns herself with chaplets of leaf and garlands of flowers, and summer spreads out its fields of waving corn, and ripe autumn lavishes its treasures in tawny, and golden, and ruddy glory over the bosom of the globe, — so long shall beauty offer herself to the gratitude and love of the gazers. It is to dishonor God to affect to despise His creation.

> "The spicy breezes
> Blow soft o'er Ceylon's isle,
> And *every prospect pleases,*
> *And only man is vile.*"

Heaven is oftentimes spoken of as the "garden of God," the garden of Eden, Paradise. There is a double reason for this, and a double meaning in it. The reasons are, first, a *fact in relation to mind*, that all our conceptions must be based on our perceptions. We can only conceive of the unknown by recalling things that are known, and then enlarging or heightening their qualities;

or uniting together qualities we have perceived separately. Our conception of heavenly beauty must be an enlargement and an exaltation of our perception of earthly beauty, or it is formless, — mere words, and no more. The second reason is *the fact in relation to heaven itself*, that there are groves and gardens, flowers and green pastures, still waters and gushing fountains there. What we have perceived of beauty here was designed to aid us, and does aid us, in the conception of the beautiful in heaven; and this conception is justified at once by our mental constitution and by the fact. The double meaning in the description is that the loveliness below is an adumbration of the loveliness above; and that our tuition in delight derived from its appreciation *here* is the preparation to our fuller appreciation of its grander manifestations hereafter.

"Te Deum Laudamus!"

# IV.

## DEATH THE GATE OF LIFE.

"Our Saviour Jesus Christ, who hath abolished death, and hath brought life and immortality to light by the Gospel." — 2 Tim. i. 10.

MAN LIFE'S GREAT PARADOX. — THE PRESENCE AND UNIVERSALITY OF DEATH. — IS DEATH A CURSE? — DEATH THE INEVITABLE CONSEQUENT OF PHYSICAL LIFE. — DEATH AS THE PENALTY OF SIN EXAMINED. — DEATH IN RELATION TO MAN. — EXAMINATION OF SCRIPTURE-TEACHINGS ON THE SUBJECT OF DEATH. — DEATH A BENEVOLENT NECESSITY. — WHAT IS DEATH? — MAN'S NATURAL AND SPIRITUAL BODIES. — PAUL'S THREE TERMS OF COMPARISON BETWEEN MAN AND GRAIN. — THE RESURRECTION OF THE NATURAL BODY CONSIDERED. — THE THREE KINDS OR DEGREES OF SUBSTANCE. — CONCLUSIONS AS TO THE REDEEMED IN HEAVEN. — SCRIPTURE TESTIMONIES AS TO THE LIFE AFTER DEATH. — DEATH SWALLOWED UP IN VICTORY. — LIFE A JOY. — DEATH A BLESSING.

MAN is life's great paradox. Animals enter without instruction into the full possession of all their instincts. The present generation learns nothing from the past, and can transmit no new intelligence to the future. The first beaver was as clever a builder, and the first bee as astute a mathematician as the last, and such they will continue forever. Life with the animal races means a certain defined condition of instinctive intelligence, from which circumstances can take little away, and to which circumstances can add as little. To defend themselves from danger, to supply their hunger, to propagate their species, to protect and provide for their young, and then to die, when the perpetuation of the species by procreation has been attained, seem to be the sole objects of their existence in relation to themselves; and to enable them to accomplish these, they are gifted with instincts, and enter without effort into their use. Man is destined to the highest greatness, and born into a state of the lowest helplessness. He has received the grandest intellectual power of all earthly creatures, and is born into the completest ignorance; —the only being possessing hopes of immortality, and the only being conscious of the certainty of death. His development is the slowest, and yet that development is to be unceasing. Through the gates of weariness and pain he ascends to knowledge; and buys, by an experience of suffering, the prudence that shall prevent suffering.

Toiling in the present, yet the past and the future belong to him;—the past by the rich legacies of its wisdom,—the future by blooming aspirations and promises. Study takes hold of and appropriates the one, and vigorous hope already seizes upon and partially makes its own of the other. Whatever the past has treasured, and whatever the future can promise, belongs to him, the heir of all the ages. But for him to inherit the past his predecessors have had to die, and to inherit the future he will himself have to die. Thus DEATH stares him in the face whichever way he turns. Experience and expectation alike reveal to him the inexorable necessity of human life. There is no escape from it. Death, as a friendly guardian, hands over to him what has been preserved of those gone before; and death, as a warden, shall unlock the portals that at present bar his attainment of what shall come after. Man stands on a narrow isthmus, with an ocean of death on either hand; his life is spent in traversing its restricted limits; and from death, learned as a certainty by what he has witnessed in others, he plunges into death, as a consciousness to himself. However appalled by the vision, his life still must relentlessly march on, and day by day the vision grows more palpable in the perception of how inevitable it is. A mysterious fascination compels him to regard it, and to regard it the more the more he shrinks from it.

The illustrations of death surround him on every hand. Every hour dies that the next may be born; each day dies and sinks into the cold, silent tomb of night that its successor may come forth: the tomb of the past is the womb of the future; the years tremble through a winter, snow-shrouded and ice-stiff, that the blue-eyed babe of spring may smile on the world that shall laugh out its glad sympathy in flowers; dust rises around him, and dust is the concrete emblem of dissolution. The soil he cultivates and the fuel he burns, the solid globe on which he treads, the clouds that float above him, are all vast cemeteries, — charnel-houses, transformed from death into new forms of life. Chemistry reveals to him the death of matter in its various decompositions; geology speaks to him out of the stony archives of the far-off past of the extinction of races; and history's long corridors and portrait-galleries are made melancholy with the mournful knell of nations, dynasties, and men past and gone. Should the lonely student of these mysteries, the solitary worshipper in these huge temples and before these high altars, cherish the wish to leave his name as one of the lights and landmarks of his times, the pallid mist of death dims the statue that ambition dreams it beholds, and the vision of greatness grows faint through the sorrowing rain of tears.

Mankind has made a great mistake in its contemplation of death, and this mistake, while being radically pursued into false assertions as to the past, has as falsely gloomed over the prospects of the future. Some have thought that death was an imperfection, — a blot on the fair face of creation, — a derangement that has entered into an otherwise perfect plan. They have believed that the primal scheme of creation comprehended no such necessity as man's dying, and that physical dissolution was only an afterthought of Divine vengeance, and inflicted as the penalty of sin. Earth, according to them, was to have been the eternal scene of man's existence, and material being the unchanging necessity of human life. From this opinion we altogether dissent. If death were not exactly coeval with life, it was life's immediate successor. For ages prior to the advent of man these two co-accessory agencies — life and death — were busy preparing the earth for that advent. There have been six grand groups or periods of animated existence, and five of these have altogether passed away, and they passed away, too, before man was created and died. Many of our rocks are solid sarcophagi. One seventh of our earth's crust is composed of limestone, and limestone is but the imbedded sepulchre of once living creatures. Whatever of this rock was beheld by the first man, was actually a monument of death. Death in inorganic nature was change, and change in the animated kingdoms was death.

Not only was there death prior to man, but there was also violent death. The larger races preyed upon the smaller, and, to build up their living tissues, the death of subsidiary races was indispensable. And what the evidence of observed facts declares to have been the case, reason can demonstrate must have been the case. Where space is limited in extent, material organizations can only increase in number up to a certain point, and then the space will be full. If increase is to continue, the decease of the old must take place to afford room for the existence of the new. Where matter is limited in quantity, and organisms are composed of matter, then, also, increase, or even continued existence, can only reach a certain point, and death must ensue; not only to furnish material for an increase of numbers, but to supply material for the continued existence of those which already exist. On the *débris* of a dead past the living present can alone stand, and the present must die to permit the existence of the future. Vegetables and animals are endowed with marvellous powers of reproduction, and were so endowed from the beginning. These powers are so prolific that any one race under favorable circumstances could speedily people the world. The fertility of reproduction is an evidence of Divine *pre*vision that death must and would occur, and it is, too, a proof of Divine *pro*vision to guard against the extinction of species resulting from the death of the individual. The bestowal of the fertility was the prophet of death. Death, therefore, was in the world before man. Man eating the fruits of the earth and the herbs of the field entailed upon them vegetable death as the necessary consequence of his existence. Death existed before him, death came with him and by him, and it is only absurd to regard physical death as the consequence of his sin.

It may be urged, that while it is certain that other creatures died prior to man's advent, yet man would not himself have physically died, unless he had sinned. It is impossible so to state this objection as that it will not involve its own contradiction. In common with all animals, man possessed at first, and still possesses, a material body. This body is subject to all the accidents and necessities to which other material bodies are subject. It must eat, or appropriate fresh matter to supply material, to repair the waste and destruction that life occasions. Life is as a fire, and the tissues are as its fuel; they must consume, and fresh substance must be appropriated to compensate the consumption. Sharing the necessities common to all material existences, man's body shared death. The reproductive powers of man, and the command to reproduce, were infallible indications of the Divine will in his case, as are these things in the case of all other animals. Reproduction was intended to be unceasing, because in the fact of each kind bringing forth their like, man's offspring would be similarly endowed with these powers. Reproduction being unceasing, in order that it might continue, death must ensue, or there would be neither space in which their offspring could exist, nor matter of which they could be composed. From the consideration of man as a physical material being, death therefore was a necessity to life, and physical death is not to be regarded as the consequence of sin.

Man is superior to the animals, not merely from the form and beauty of the body, but in the possession of spiritual being. This spiritual being is his immortal part. But for the full development of this spiritual being earth is an incompetent, and would ever have been an incompetent plane. It is only adapted for being, and was only designed to be, the school of his preparation, the lower forms where he might become fitted for the more glorious universities on high. If death were the end of existence, and life were dwarfed down to the twin boundaries of the cradle and the grave, then death were indeed a disorder, a derangement of a wise plan. Regarding death as only the introduction to a new state, man is still life's great paradox; but if we were to regard death as the fatal terminus of life's toilsome journey, then man would be nature's most insoluble problem. He would alone be the startling exception to what all observation teaches us, — that indications of universal fitness in things are the evidences of a universal design. The disproportion which exists between man's capacity for improvement, and the small opportunities his earth-life affords him for improvement, — between his ability to acquire knowledge, and the brief term allowed here for its acquisition, — between his almost boundless desires and their limited satisfaction, — between his hopes and his destiny, if death be the cessation of identity; this disproportion is so immense, that it would be out of harmony with all the chorus of testimony to the existence of design that swells up from all other created things. It would teach us at once to doubt of there being any Divine wisdom presiding in the universe; or, rather, the perception of the disproportion would overmaster doubt as to man's future existence; and even though it were false that man would continue to live after death, it would yet compel us to believe the falsehood despite of the evidence that it was such.

Many have adopted the notion of natural death being the penalty of sin, from the literal language of the word of God, and their belief in it may be unassailable while their mistaken reading of the Bible remains uncorrected. On this head, the following brief considerations are suggested. I. The Bible does certainly use the words "death" and "dead" in two senses, — the one meaning *natural* decease, the death of the body, — and the other signifying *spiritual* death; not the dissolution of the soul, but such a state of antagonism to God as to render the soul non-receptive of God's blessings, and which perverts into everlasting misery the life which the Creator designed to be an everlasting joy. Only in this way can be understood the promises, "He that liveth and believeth in me shall *never die*";[1] "He that believeth in me shall not come into condemnation, but *is passed from death unto life*";[2] "If a man keep my sayings, he shall never see death":[3] and such statements as, "for this my son was *dead*, and is alive

[1] John xi. 26. [2] John v. 24. [3] John viii. 51.

again"; or, "Ye who were *dead* in trespasses and sins, yet hath he quickened";[1] "The *soul* that sinneth it shall *die*";[2] "I know thy works, that thou hast a name to live, and art *dead*";[3] "Enlighten mine eyes, lest I sleep the sleep of *death*";[4] etc. II. Jesus came to annul the penalty of sin, and redeem man from the curse: "Jesus Christ hath *abolished death*, and brought life and immortality to light by the Gospel."[5] The death that he abolished was the death of the curse. He did not abolish natural death, therefore natural death was not the death of the curse. The death that He hath abolished is spiritual death, therefore spiritual death, the death of the soul, was the death of the curse. "As in Adam all die, so in Christ shall all be made alive";[6] the life we may have in Christ is not the perpetuation of our natural existence, therefore the death we suffer in Adam was not natural decease. "The wages of sin is death; but the gift of God is eternal life, through Jesus Christ our Lord."[7] The death and life here contradistinguished are mutual opposites: the life we are to receive through Christ is spiritual life; and the death we have undergone through Adam is spiritual death. III. The same conclusion must be arrived at from the consideration of the narrative in Genesis: "In the

[1] Eph. ii. 1.
[2] Ezek. xviii. 4.
[3] Rev. iii. 1.
[4] Ps. xiii. 3.
[5] 2 Tim. i. 10.
[6] 1 Cor. xv. 22.
[7] Rom. vi. 23.

day that thou eatest thereof, thou shalt surely die." That Adam did not naturally die *that day*, the narrative asserts; nor can the words be interpreted that he "became *subject to death* from that day." If natural death was the penalty, nine hundred and thirty years of life is rather a long interval between the announcement of the penalty and its fulfilment. Either the word "day," or the word "death," must be understood in a non-literal sense. "The soul that sinneth, *it* shall die," seems to indicate that the death of the soul, and not the decease of the body, is and was the penalty of sin. This conclusion, confirmed as it is by the narrative itself, is the only one that is consistent with the whole tenor of the Scriptures, and it renders the whole tenor of the Scriptures consistent with the facts of science and the deductions of philosophy. Natural death, therefore, is not the penalty of sin, but the necessary condition of a continued material existence.

While death is a necessity of life, yet it is a benevolent necessity. In its establishment God has only proven Himself a more beneficent Father as well as a wiser contriver. To learn the reasons for the appointment of death, and the consequences resulting from it, will only exalt His claims upon human gratitude, as it will also afford us a grander spectacle of His more comprehensive design. Earth will be seen to be the seminary of heaven; and the decease of former generations was only contrived to admit of the existence of new generations, whose home and abiding-place is above. Thus, and thus only, is secured the accomplishment of the promise, "Of the increase of his kingdom there shall be no end."

A man dies: —

"Life and thought have gone away
Side by side,
Leaving door and windows wide:
Careless tenants they!
All within is dark as night:
In the windows is no light;
And no murmur at the door,
So frequent on its hinge before."

In this wreck and desolation, what is it that has died? Evidently only the body. "Ashes to ashes, and dust to dust," is the solemn requiem uttered as to *that*. It was a marvellous combination of earthly substances, held together by a still more wondrous thing that we call "life"; the bond that held them together is broken, so back to their original elements the substances of the body return. Decomposition shall prepare them for recomposition, in order that the vast cycle of human existence may ceaselessly go on. The body dies because the real man is withdrawn from it. The body was an accident; — however necessary to his birth as an individual, yet not necessary to his continued existence. Through all the manifold and perpetual changes of the body, the man continued the same being, and he continues the same being despite the last great change of death.

Then, what survives death? The Apostle answers the question, "We know that if our earthly house of this tabernacle be dissolved, we have a building of God, a house not made with hands, eternal in the heavens. For in this we groan, earnestly desiring to be clothed upon with our house which is from heaven. . . . . Not that we would be unclothed, but clothed upon, that mortality might be swallowed up of life. . . . . Knowing that while we are in the body, we are absent from the Lord; and we are willing to be absent from the body, and to be present with the Lord."[1] Absence from the body does not, therefore, destroy the identity or the consciousness of the man. But the preservation of our consciousness and identity necessitates the preservation of our human form, and even of our individual human forms. The man whose body is dead must still remain *a man;* not a mere spark of life, a flickering flame of being, but an actual and distinct existence, a human being conscious of his own identity, responsible for his previous conduct, and cognizant of God's presence. But form implies substance, for form is but the limitation of substance: and substance in form implies body. Man must, consequently, possess two bodies, one the *material*, which dies, — and one a *spiritual* body, which survives the dissolution of the other.

[1] 2 Cor. v. 1-8.

We have previously seen that spirits are substantial men, not composed of earthly, but of spiritual and never-dying substance; and the Apostle has devoted a large portion of his First Epistle to the Corinthians to elucidate this subject. In it he declares, "There is a natural body, and there is a spiritual body,"[1] and further asserts that "the natural body is sown, and the spiritual body rises." He very felicitously compares the sowing, death, and rising of man, to the sowing, death, and germination of grain. This comparison is so complete that it deserves minute consideration. The Apostle makes use of three terms in relation to both man and grain; and to fix the analogy it will be necessary to determine the resemblance of each term. We begin with the middle phrase. The death of the grain symbolizes the death of the man. Both must die before they can rise. But the *sowing*, the first term, must take place before the death of either. This shows that the sowing of the grain cannot be analogous to the burial of man's dead body; and this for several reasons; first, the *man* is not present in the body when that is interred,—we inter *it* only because *he* is no longer there; and, secondly, the sowing takes place *before* death, according to the Apostle, whereas interment does not take place till *after* death. A further reason why the Apostle cannot have designed to compare the sowing of the grain to the

[1] 1 Cor. xv. 35-50.

interment of the dead body, is that many dead bodies are not interred at all. And a still further reason is, that the third term of the comparison will be altogether frustrated by the assignment of such an interpretation to the first.

What portion of man's history is it, then, we ask, which is analogous to the sowing of the grain? The Apostle is speaking of *man's* being sown, not of any sowing of man's body. We answer, man is sown into the world when he is born into the world, just as the grain is sown into the earth when placed there. The man is sown by birth into the world in order that *he* may die, just as the grain is sown into the earth, *its world*, in order that *it* may die. The whole of the description is strikingly apposite to this interpretation. In a far higher than a mere gross, material sense, man is sown in "corruption, dishonor, weakness," when, as a natural body, he enters by birth into the world. The "sowing" is the beginning of man's earth-life, or life on the earth; and the hereditary propensities to evil, the lusts of sense, and the frivolities of time, render it far too often and too much a whole scene of corruption, dishonor, and weakness.

Man's death is compared to the death of the grain. This comparison is exactly accurate. In the grain it is only the husk that dies. With the man it is only the husk — the natural body, the physical envelope — that dies. When the husk of the grain dies, the germ of new life has sprouted forth; and when the physical envelope of the man dies, the spiritual being is released from it and ascends. It is necessary that the grain should be sown that it may die, and it is necessary that it should both be sown and die that the germ of new life may ascend into the bright light and warm sunshine above its earthly resting-place. And, in like manner, man must be born that he may die, and both be born and die in order that he may rise a spiritual, immortal being. The providential purpose in the implantation of the germ of life within the grain was, that by dying a more munificent life might be developed; and the great design in the birth of man was, that by dying a nobler existence might be attained. The enlarged multiplication of the species, as the result of the death of the grain, is the symbol of the enhanced development of the powers and privileges, the gifts and the glory of human existence, to be realized in the other life.

The third term requires consideration. Not only are they alike sown and do they die alike, but there is a further resemblance in the quickening of the man and the germination of the grain. The dead husk and starchy substance of the grain do not rise; but the living germ, from the husk, the living principle, from the body of the seed. So, in like manner, man's spirit rises from the dead body; its ascent from the body is the cause and sign of death. The dead husk wastes away in the soil, and the dead body moulders back to dust. The life-germ in both cases has no further need of the outer envelope it wore, and can put it to no further use. Without it, both the sprouting stem of wheat and the risen spirit of man are more glorious things than they were before.

Sometimes this comparison of the Apostle is regarded as illustrating a fancied resurrection of *the dead body;* but this view is evidently wrong. It illustrates most felicitously the resurrection of the living man from the dead body; but to attempt to interpret it otherwise renders the comparison singularly inapt. The germination of a seed is not the resuscitation of the dead husk, the covering of the germ; and the resurrection of *the man* is not any resuscitation of the body. The germination of the grain is the bursting up of its inner living principle into a more beautiful and a new form of existence; and the resurrection of the man is the rising up of his living principle, his spirit, into a new and grander existence. Consequently, the Apostle has been really treating of the resurrection of the man from the dead body, not of the resuscitation of the dead body itself. The impersonal pronoun "it," used in our translation of the passage (1 Cor. xv. 42–44), is not used or implied in the Greek. The *man* has been clothed with a mortal, a natural body, "the earthly house of this tabernacle," and the *man* is raised an "incorruptible, immortal, spiritual body," or has put on "the house not made with hands, the building of God, eternal in the heavens."

Addressing some who believed in the old Hebrew and Egyptian idea of the resurrection of the dead body, the Apostle declares in the same chapter, "Thou fool; that which thou sowest, thou sowest NOT that body that shall be";[1] for, as he asserts again, "Flesh and blood cannot inherit the kingdom of God, neither doth corruption inherit incorruption";[2] or, as he more emphatically expresses it, "the natural body is sown, and *the spiritual body is raised.*"[3] He no more means that the dead natural body shall at some future day be sublimated and transformed into a spiritual body, than he intends to teach that the dead husk of the grain shall be transformed into the living plant. *That* is dead and done with, and dead because done with; and up from the dead husk or body the living principle rises. The birth, death, and resurrection of the man, and the sowing, death, and germination of the grain are thus mutually representative; and the comparison of the Apostle is justified and borne out even into details. In both, death is, therefore, the gate of life.

What intermission, asks the soul yearning after life, is there between our conscious existence in this world and the commencement of our consciousness in the next? Believers in the dogma of the

[1] 1 Cor. xv. 36, 37. [2] ver 50. [3] ver. 44.

resurrection of the dead body have had to invent what the Word of God does not justify them in the invention of, a strange sort of nondescript middle state, filling up the period elapsing between the decease of the body and its future resurrection; while yet they were baffled by many passages of Scripture that would not harmonize with their hypothesis. Much extravagant speculation has been wasted upon this middle state, and the wildest notions have been hazarded, when nothing is simpler than the formula, "a natural body for the natural world, and for the spiritual world a spiritual body."

The root of all errors on this subject has been in the definition given to spirit. It has been so long called *immaterial*, that almost all idea of substantiality has been banished from ordinary conceptions of it. We can, however, have no idea of the existence of something that is not substantial. There are three degrees of substance, each discretely different from the others, different as to qualities and properties, but still substance. These three are, — material substance, which forms the lowest class in existence; spiritual substance, which forms the middle link in the chain of being; and Divine substance, which is God. The spirit is immaterial, that is, its substance is altogether discrete from *matter;* but it is only a lax use of words which confounds the idea of immateriality with that of unsubstantiality. That which has form must have substance, as that only which is substance can possess form. Without form, existence is impossible; for existence is only the form which the essence assumes. To say that a spirit is without substance, is to say, therefore, that a spirit has no existence, that it is not; or, as an acute writer expresses it, "that it is NO-THING, existing NO-WHERE and NO-WHEN."

The Word of God unmistakably conducts us to the conclusion that spirits are bodies, substantial, and possessing form; and leads us most satisfactorily to believe that there is no such thing as *disembodied* spirits, and no such place as the middle state of existence, such as that surmised between the death of the material body and its resuscitation. Moses was certainly dead, and yet on the Mount of Transfiguration the three disciples beheld him ministering to the Lord Jesus.[1] The two angels who appeared to John, and who declared themselves to be prophets,[2] were substantial beings possessing form. The thousands rescued out of every "kindred, and tongue, and people, and nation,"[3] were substantial beings in the human form. These had certainly lived on earth, they had as certainly died on earth, and yet as certainly they possessed substantial bodies, which the Apostle could see, just as they also could behold each other, and together praise the Lamb.

Two important conclusions, however, result from the foregoing observations. First, there are only

[1] Matt. xvii. 3. [2] Rev. xix. 10; xxii. 9. [3] Rev. v. 9.

two kinds of bodies spoken of in the Bible, the one kind *natural* bodies, which remain on earth, matter to matter, or dust to dust; and the other kind *spiritual* bodies, which belong to the spiritual world. There are no others than these. These beatified men did not possess natural bodies, for these they had left behind when they quitted the material world; therefore, the only conclusion remaining to us is, that they were *spiritual* bodies. Their substantiality was spiritual substance, or, in other words, they were spiritual bodies.

But, secondly, the existence of man as a spiritual body is spoken of as being the result of *resurrection*. Hence, as these did possess such spiritual bodies, their resurrection must have already taken place. Consequently, the resurrection rightly understood is not the resuscitation of the dead material body, but the raising of the spiritual body from the dead natural body. There was to them no middle state of existence, they had already entered into their "eternal house," "absent from the body" they were "present with the Lord," and had joined the "spirits of just men made perfect." To precisely the same conclusion are we led by the parable of Dives and Lazarus.[1] Both Lazarus and Dives were spiritual bodies, substantial beings in the human form, and at once, without any middle state, Lazarus went to his own place, and Dives to the place he also had made his own.

[1] Luke xvi. 19 – 30.

The great impassable gulf was eternally fixed between them. There was to be no common ground on which they might in future stand together; their resurrection had been realized, and henceforth were they to continue to exist spiritual beings in the spiritual world, the one in heaven and the other in hell.

Exactly similar is the declaration made by the Lord: "Now that the dead are raised, even Moses showed at the bush, when he called the Lord the God of Abraham, the God of Isaac, and the God of Jacob. For he is not a God of the dead, but of the living: for all live unto him."[1] This magnificent statement declares several things. 1. That, as seen by the Lord, there is no such thing as a dead *man;* or that the death of the body is not the decease of the *man.* 2. That the dead *are* raised; not that they shall be, or may hope to be raised, but that the resurrection of the dead is a fact now taking place,—the raising of the man from the dead body. 3. That this resurrection was taking place in the days of Abraham and Isaac and Jacob, for they had then been "raised." 4. That Moses was, to some extent, conscious of the certainty of this fact. 5. That the apparently simple expression of God being the God of Abraham, Isaac, and Jacob, is at the same time a divinely-given testimony to the fact of their continued existence, and a prophetic declaration that the "heirs to the prom-

[1] Luke xx. 37, 38.

ises" shall in like manner be raised, when it shall please the Divine Wisdom to call them *home* to Himself.

Some of those thus raised are spoken of by the Apostle as "the spirits of just men made perfect."[2] Now if they were already perfect, it must be folly to presume that they are enjoying only a moiety of existence, pining in longing anticipation for a reunion with their to-be-resuscitated material bodies, which in their old earthly state they rejoiced to cast away.

The term resurrection, or "rising again," no more implies the resuscitation of the dead body than does being "born again" imply the re-entrance into the world through the womb of the mother. Nicodemus misunderstood the one, and many persons appear only able to misunderstand the other expression. Man rises from the dead; it is only the body that is *dead;* and resurrection, therefore, is man's rising from the dead body.

This view of the resurrection renders it universal, immediate, and certain. It abolishes the intellectual nightmare of a middle condition of disembodiment; it strips death of all the dark imaginations with which it has been invested: as the Scriptures teach us, "it *abolishes death,*" for "death is swallowed up in victory"; and through the Gospel "life and immortality are brought to life." The babe born this morning has entered upon

[1] Heb. xii. 23.

the possession of a life which can never be destroyed. God has formed it so far in His image as to have endowed it henceforth with the attribute of eternal being. Its existence for weal or woe is now an unalterable fact; it is now a pillar that can never be thrown down; a flame that can never be extinguished. Mutations may and must pass over it in the career of its pilgrimage below; the great mutation of physical death must be endured at the end thereof; but the being still lives on, and will live on forever, an identity never to be merged into that of any other being, and a consciousness that shall never be lost. That little babe struggling with feeble cries, with the breath for the first time distending its lungs, is a marvellous thing, a sublime spectacle, a stupendous and eternal fact.

Life is a joy, and the culmination of the joy of life is the certainty that it is indestructible. In this joy of life we may feel strong and buoyant; and, though there are dark riddles that we cannot read aright in this lower plane of life's manifestation, tortuous mazes among which we wander, mysterious problems we cannot solve, sorrows we cannot soothe, wrongs we cannot redress, and misery that we can do so little to alleviate, yet the certainty of eternal life being within us, nerves the pinions of hope to sweep forward to the realities of the second chapter of the book of being, to unriddle and set right the problems and wrongs of the first. He in whom this sublime consciousness is awakened can confide in the compensations that must be provided, and the workings of which we shall one day be able to comprehend. The veil that covers the face of Isis, the mysteries of Divine Wisdom in mundane things, may not be removed by the hand of mortal, but this mortality shall put on immortality; our life shall robe itself in garments as immortal as itself, and then the veil shall melt away from before the vision of the soul. Life is a joy, and the more fully conscious we become of our life, the greater becomes the joy. Earth's "muddy vestments of decay," this "mortal coil," frustrate and diminish this consciousness. Only at rare intervals, and for brief periods, do we enter into the higher potencies and principles of our own nature, and even then the body with its material necessities and weight and feebleness bears us down. Our souls are in a double sense chained to earth, both as a physical and mental fact. Death is the deliverer, which enfranchises the spirit from its prison-house. Then death is a blessing.

We solemnly ask ourselves the question, What does death in reality do? And Death, rightly heard, answers us, "I find the body feeble and worn-out, crippling the young limbs of the soul, fettering its higher soarings, blinding the soul's eager sight, benumbing the stretched ears that strive to catch the inner harmonies of creation, wearying the laborious thought, congealing the struggling utterance, and investing the warm affections with the impotence of dust, and I strip the gyves away. I burst the bars of the prison, and throw down the doors, that the soul may ascend to liberty. Man in the body is as the chrysalis concealed in the grub. I rend the pupa case that the psyche may come forth. My work is only the pulling down of the scaffolding, that the building may be discovered, — only the breaking of the ground-glass globe, that the light may shine forth in its undimmed brightness, — only drawing the dazzling blade from the hiding sheath that it may be kissed by the sunbeams which it reflects back to heaven, — only the opening of the green bud, that the full-bosomed flower may appear. Men have feared me and slandered me. They have painted me as a grizzly wreck of being, a dart-armed monster revelling in the misery I make, my coming a horror, and my work a cruelty. They have slandered me! A reaper among the young flowers, the blossoms which I gather I bear upwards to heaven. A gleaner among the ears that are left on the ground, and I garner the grain to God!"

And our hearts reply that death is a warder, flinging open the gates that barrier the path of mortality to immortality; a white-wanded usher, introducing man to the sublimer associates of the heavenly assembly; our guide over the slender bridge that spans the gulf between this life and the next; the great revealer, lifting the dark screen that has long concealed what we have so eagerly desired to behold; the angel of loving mien, bidding the sorrowful to weep no more, and whispering to the weary to rest. Because life is a joy, and because death is only the introduction of man into a higher and fuller life, therefore *death is a blessing.**

* For a further elucidation of the subject of the Resurrection, the reader is respectfully referred to a lecture entitled, "Will the Natural Body Rise?" Third Edition. Pitman: Paternoster Row, London.

# V.

## DO THE DEPARTED FORGET US?

"Then he said, I pray thee therefore, father, that thou wouldest send him to my father's house: for I have five brethren." — LUKE xvi. 27, 28.

HUMAN NECESSITY TO LOVE AND BE BELOVED. — THE LAW OF LOVE. — THE QUESTIONS THAT LOVE ASKS AS TO THE BELOVED WHO HAVE GONE. — THE EARTH-LIFE THE BEGINNING OF MAN'S EXISTENCE. — WHAT MAN TAKES WITH HIM INTO THE OTHER LIFE. — NO NECESSARY FORGETFULNESS IN THE OTHER LIFE, NOR CESSATION OF LOVE FOR THOSE LOVED WHILE ON EARTH. — SCRIPTURE TESTIMONIES. — NEED OF DEEPER VIEWS. — TEMPORAL UNIONS AND TEMPORARY ATTACHMENTS. — ONLY REAL AND PROFOUND LOVE PERMANENT. — LOVE THE CAUSE OF REMEMBRANCE. — THE BLESSINGS OF FORGETFULNESS. — THE ARGUMENT FROM EXPERIENCE. — THE FULNESS OF HEAVENLY JOY.

NO human heart is satisfied with loving without being beloved in return. The more sensitive the heart, the stronger will be its craving to love and to be beloved. The depth of the devotion which it feels may be measured by the urgency of its need for the reciprocation of its love. It is only because of the infinitude and universality of the Divine love that God desires an instituted and universal love from man. Jesus was hungry for the devotion of those for whom He proved His love by laying down His life. In every act of the Divine providence God exhibits His love, and therefore seeks that man's love for Him may be shown in all that he does.

Man is so formed that *loving* shall constitute his real happiness. He may be happy because he may love. All joy is so much the result of love, that the one may be measured by the other. Delight is experienced in the manifestation of the love previously felt as an emotion of the soul; because for love to express itself is to add a more sentient reality to the consciousness of loving. Therefore the reciprocation of love is necessary to human happiness. Unless our love be returned, our love itself cannot grow and be developed. It will be dwarfed and stultified, and will perish of inanition. The intensest human affection cannot continually withstand utter indifference. Love's manifestations must be accepted by the object of its devotion, and their acceptance promotes the increase of those manifestations. By becoming more and more active in its expression, love becomes increasingly active as a passion in the lover.

It is the very nature of love to desire that the beloved should be happy. Not only that they shall be happy, but love also desires to promote that happiness; that is, to be active in contributing to their increased happiness. Our love yearns to be the cause of additional delight to our loved ones, of delight that they could not have experienced without the love of the lover. This is the craving of the truly loving soul. But without the reciprocation of our love, this craving can never be satisfied; for the love fades and withers under the consciousness that it is not a means of imparting enhanced felicity to the beloved. Then it is like a potent spring, that might have become a joy-giving river, caverned at its source; a pent-in fire that must needs smoulder and be extinguished for lack of the free winds to blow upon it. The choice food on which love lives is its delightful manifestations, and without these, love languishes, starves, and dies.

But some, many, of our loved ones have departed from this world, and yet we cease not to love them. We desire to continue to love them, though they have gone out from our presence. We desire, too, that they should love us still, in order that our own love for them may not droop and pass away. Therefore there is a tender melancholy and a deep yearning of the soul as we ask ourselves, Do the departed forget us? Our love for them is eager for the answer. Do they love there still? Not only can they reflect, and can they love, but do they remember *us?* and do they love *us* still? The continuance of the departed as rational and free beings proves their possession of the power to think and their power to love; but what we long to know is, whether death, that removes them from our sight, also removes us from their recollection. Life is sweetened and made delicious by love and friendship, and, although God is very merciful in providing us with objects whom it is our happiness and privilege to hold in tenderest affection, yet we cannot so far estrange ourselves from our bygones as to forget those whose passage has preceded our own into the spiritual world. The joy which our remembrance of such friends occasions us compels us to believe that their remembrance of us would cause joy to them, if our positions were reversed, were we departed and had they remained. The purer and better we become, the deeper and tenderer is the delight that our consciousness drinks in from the fountains of memory. By their transit into that other world they have become purer and better, and we are forced to inquire how much of their joy consists in mentally retraversing the scenes they knew and once loved, and re-collecting the reminiscences of those whom once they knew and cherished.

Some have contended that as our entrance into this world was "a waking and a forgetting," so our entrance into the next may be similarly an oblivion as to this; and that therefore we are as absent unto them as they are unto us. But to say they forget us is to render us still more absent unto them; for we can still remember and love them.

In reply, we may state that no argument worthy attentive or serious consideration has ever been produced in favor of the existence of man as an individual identity prior to his birth into this world.

The idea itself has only had life enough in it to become reproduced as a sort of a vague allusion by a few poets. It is the corollary of the doctrine of metempsychosis, and the *reductio ad absurdum* of Monboddo's theory of the "origin of species," or Darwin's hypothesis of "natural selection." Every consideration tends to show that our earth-life is the beginning of our identity. Whatever may have been the condition of the spiritual particles which enter into the constitution of MYSELF, their aggregation as MYSELF was not realized until my birth into this, the lowest plane of rational existence. That ME has remained unchanged, notwithstanding all mental developments by exercise, and improvement by education. Though that ME, or my consciousness of identity, has passed through manifold alterations as to intellectual forms of thought, conceptions of manners, principles of morals, or doctrines of religion, yet this consciousness of identity has continued unaffected by all such subsidiary changes. They were changes taking place within my consciousness of identity, but not of that consciousness. Nor has the displacement of the particles that formed my physical body in my infancy and youth, and their replacement by the particles which constitute my present body, at all affected my consciousness of identity. Revelation and reason teach me that after death I shall still continue to exist. The continuation of *my* existence is the continued existence of the ME, this consciousness of my own identity; for, to remain the same being, I must preserve this consciousness of the same identity. There is, therefore, no parallel between our birth into *this*, and our entrance into *that* world. Into this I entered physically and mentally a babe,— into that I shall enter substantially and mentally a *man*.

There are many important consequences resulting from this difference, and some of them bear a direct relevancy to our immediate subject. Man takes into the other life all his intellectual and affectional nature, such as, by his inner and outer life, he has made it. Not only is the spirit, newly entered into the spiritual world, the same being as to his consciousness of identity, but he is also the same being in his loves and thoughts there as he was here. Changes, and those vast ones, must necessarily await him in the unveiling processes of eternity; but such as he is when he leaves this plane of existence, such is he when he enters *that*. Now the love for friends, and remembrance of them, are things of the soul, and they are no more destroyed by the transition from this into that state, than are the other faculties of the spirit and the mental results of their exercise. We may conclude then, that *at first* our departed cease not to remember and cease not to love us. There is no *immediate* obliteration of recollection, and no *necessary* cessation of love.

If there be, and no doubt there is in many cases, an oblivion that will enwrap their memories of their earth-friends, and with this, of consequence, an expiration of love for them, it will result from the operation of other laws, and the coming into activity of other principles in the natures of those who have gone before us.

The Word of God clearly intimates that there is no *necessary* forgetfulness, and at least suggests the universality of the fact that recognition of friends in the other life may be possible. In the parable of Dives and Lazarus, which has frequently been referred to in the course of this little work, because it is so full of instruction on these subjects, the Lord describes Dives as remembering the fact of the existence of his five brethren, and as still feeling sufficient love for them to induce him to pray Abraham to send Lazarus to his father's house.[1] This instance is rendered still more remarkable by the fact that Dives is described as being, not a happy and blessed spirit, but as being in hell, and there lifting "up his eyes, being in torment," as showing that not even his dreadful condition could obliterate the remembrance of, or destroy his interest in, and anxiety concerning, his five brethren on earth. Not only did he remember the fact of his having had five brethren, but the further fact that they were all still remaining in the world he had quitted, and the yet further

[1] Luke xvi. 27, 28.

fact that they would be found in his "father's house." The answer of Abraham to a prior request of Dives is equally illustrative of the fact that those on the other side are certainly, on their first arriving into the spiritual world, able to remember what took place in this. "Son, *remember* that thou in thy lifetime receivedst thy good things, and Lazarus evil things."[1] And a similar testimony to the general remembrance possessed by those in the spiritual world may be found in the fact that Abraham knew that men in the world had "Moses and the prophets,"[2] although this fact could only have been communicated to him. It assuredly is not too much to assert that this parable justifies us in these inferences, which it is so calculated to suggest that the marvel would be if they escaped us.

The belief of recognition of the departed is also intimated in those tenderly sad words of David, as to the little son whom he had so loved, so mourned, and temporarily lost,—"I shall go to him, although he shall not return to me."[3] The inference is at least warranted by a rational consideration of the Scriptures, that Moses and Elias, who ministered to the Lord on the Mount of Transfiguration, as well as the two prophets, who had become angels, and who ministered unto John the Revelator, had not forgotten, nor had ceased to feel a loving interest in the earth upon which they

[1] Luke xvi. 25. [2] ver. 20. [3] 2 Sam. xii. 23.

had lived, the scene of their former labors, revisited on these occasions in glory. It must be a source of consolation to all earnest lovers of their race to think, that as angels they may not only preserve their recollection of and their interest in mankind on earth, but that they may be in a position to promote their welfare, and to render them loving aid and comfort.

Yet we must take deeper and more comprehensive views than those indicated above. On earth there is necessarily much association between persons strangely dissimilar in tastes and dispositions. There are incongruous friendships, superficial and physical attachments, and connections whose only basis and motive is convenience or worldly gain. Many seemingly ardent affections are only *seeming*, affectations of love from which the deeper feelings of the heart wander away, and into which the secret thoughts never enter. Oil and water have met but have never blended, and can never blend. As external circumstances alone brought such into association, so a change even in external circumstances would sever the transient attachment, and estrange the superficially united lovers. The affinity was but partial, and the union could only be temporary. Between married partners this is far too often the case. The love of such was no more than a transient feeling, a fancy, the charm of which has fled, leaving only the thrall of a bondage that was endured with impatience, till the death of one of the twain that terminates it becomes welcomed with a sense of relief.

Between brothers and sisters their affection is often only of this external kind, the consequence of association and a vague expression of the love which all are created to feel and desire. Any other person would have formed an object of regard equally attractive, and for whom their love would have been equally deep, or rather equally shallow. Unfortunately, too, for man, soul-friendships are similarly rare. The story of Damon and Pythias has but few originals and few imitators. Even in families, although the parents may strive to evince no partiality in their conduct to their children, yet it is the inevitable law of soul that they like best those who are most like them; and perhaps the more spiritual the affections of the parents, the more operative in them will this law be. The general feeling of love for their children, *as such*, will enable them to love them generally alike; but with some there will be a closer intimacy, a fuller communion of spirit, and a tenderer sympathy. We need not regret this, and we cannot prevent it; for there is a law of spiritual consociation to which we are subject, and over which we can have no control. Every Abraham has his Isaac; Jacob is not alone in his love for Joseph; nor was David the only father who has mourned over his Absalom. It is only the spiritual side of the world-wide fact of chemical affinity. The latter is the physical expression, and the former the spiritual expression of the same universal law of "like cleaving unto like."

Love, then, is of an internal or an external kind; the one is the creature of circumstances, but the other no circumstances can altogether overcome. Even here on earth we can see illustrations of this fact. Two sons will leave their home and journey to foreign lands, one will forget the old roof-tree and those it may shelter, while the other will wander back again to watch and guard the declining days of his parents, to be the family stay, their comfort and their hope. In the other life the same law must have place, and operate yet more markedly. The external, the shallow, the transitory affection must and will pass away, and with it the recollection which love alone could keep fresh. Only the internal, the real, the permanent, will remain. It seems almost like a mere play upon words, but it is not a repetition. The words form a series, and each is the effect of the former: because the love is internal, it is real; because real, it is necessarily permanent, and therefore must remain; because it is interwoven with the very life, and is the inevitable consequence of the very nature of the individual, it will endure. Only those who are really *lovers*, therefore, will continue to love, and their love will be the source of their remembrance.

There are conjunctions which embrace, or are

common to, many, and there are soul-unions that are limited to a few. Within the wider circles of these common conjunctions there may exist many smaller circles of such soul-unions. It is only another illustration of the proverb, "wheels within wheels," another exemplification of the great fact which can also be seen in all society, and of which the sublimest natural symbol is the inter-movements of the heavenly bodies; each planet with its statellites performing their mutual and lesser orbits, amid the regular and orderly processions of all the suns and planets of the universe. These conjunctions that are common revolve around some common centre, — political parties round political doctrines, philosophic sects round philosophic schools, or religious denominations around some one great Teacher. So far as these objects are limited to earth, so far such conjunctions are equally restricted. So far as such consociations really enter into, mould, and lay hold of men's inmost natures, only so far can such conjunctions be permanent in the other life. Like will seek for its like, and what we *are* will rule our love for what is like to ourselves. Hence real conjunction can only exist between those who genuinely love each other; and such love is the result of our actual natures, such as they were originally by parentage, and such as they have subsequently become by the moulding processes of education. Where such conjunction exists, forgetfulness is impossible. As the panting hart seeks the water-brooks, so the soul will yearn for its beloved. With such, recognition is inevitable. As the gazer recognizes his reflected image in the mirror, so the soul will recognize its like. With such, separation is equally impossible. The thought of the mind will speed the willing spirit to the side of the being thought of, and their changeless love will conjoin them forever.

Love is the mystery of man's nature half revealed to him. Heart-unions are marvellous things, and potent for good and evil. There is no more expressive word in our language than *attachment*, which literally means *binding together*. Hearts attached are blendings of the springs of life, the waters from which must ever afterwards seek to form an undivided stream. The more those attachments are genuine and profound, the more indissoluble are the ties that they establish. When they are the most real and most profound, they are wrapped up with human destiny, to be parts of us forever. Such beloved ones have, and everlastingly will have, power over us, and over such loving ones shall we forever have power. Their love for us will draw them near to us, as our love for them will impel us toward them; and being made one with us by love, as angels we may together be made one in the Lord by our common love for Him. There is an individual application as well as a societary and general signification in the words, "They went out *from* us because they were not *of* us."

It must be understood that nothing in the foregoing asserts more than the immutability of the soul's affections after death. During this life the whole bent and purpose of a man's soul as to *good* and *evil* can become changed by regeneration. The *de*formed may become *re*formed, and the *mal*formed may become *trans*formed by this mighty process, afforded and effected by the mercy of the Lord. It is the vast engine permitted to man by which he can determine his own destiny, and, within certain limits, change his character. Though, as previously shown, regeneration accomplishes the removal of *defects* of character, not of differences; for *differences* are not defects. Man has attachments that more or less profoundly unite him to their objects; and what is here asserted is, that only those that are profound can be permanent. This law of remembrance, recognition, and association in the future life is altogether merciful. It is to be regarded as a fact, unhappily too possible, that heaven may become the abiding-place of some members of a family, of one of a married couple, of one of a pair of friends; while the desolations of hell may be the condition of the others. If recollection of our earthly associations were universal and permanent, heaven would not be a tearless and sorrowless abode, while the mother could remember her lost child, the wife her lost husband, the child its parents, the friend his friend. The warmer their love for the lost ones, the more intense would be the pang of misery caused by their absence from them; so that the highest qualities of the saved would thus become to them the source of their deepest anguish. The more worthy of heaven by their tenderness, the less of a heaven would they possess, were it not for this blessing of forgetfulness, because of love seeking its beloved and lost, or wasting itself in sighs when all its researches were vain. There would again be "Rachel weeping for her children, and would not be comforted because they are not." No; it is better to think that such love as shall not be made permanent in heaven was only of a temporary, transient, superficial kind, — only the result of earthly association, and therefore only the creature of time, to be quenched in the brightness of heaven's glory, to be fused away as dross from the pure gold of the nature of the glorified man, who then will love only that which their clearer perceptions show to be worthy of their love, and in devotion to which they will find an ever-increasing joy.

Perhaps this thought may sadden at first sight, but it will be only at first sight. Even if it be otherwise, it would still be better that our brief earth-life should be darkened by a mournful cloud than that such a cloud should wrap us with its shadows forever. But it need not thus afflict us. Could we see the inmost natures of those whom we think that we love here, we could only really love *our like.* As they approached more or less nearly to our own natures, the spiritual conjunction between us and them would be more or less intimate, and more or less remote. Pity for them, interest in their welfare, and the desire to help them, might still prompt our tender offices, as these emotions prompt the tender offices of angels toward even the hapless infernals; but such emotions would not be *love.* Defect of perception may, therefore, deceive us, or suffer us to deceive ourselves, into believing that the feeling we experience is genuine love, when in reality it is only its semblance. As our knowledge of others, and our acquaintance with ourselves, enlarges even here, we sometimes wake up to the perception that what we have, in boyish days, fancied to be the profoundest affection was not such. Those who were the heroines of the romantic dreams of our childhood are not now able to stir the pulses to a quicker beat, nor to inspire the soul with a single feeling warmer than respect. Such small experience is only the foregleam of what we may anticipate will more fully come hereafter, when only love shall be the fount of memory and the law of association.

In this life the discovery of such facts may have a tendency to make us "sadder although wiser men," and to incline us to feel "I 'm aweary, aweary"; but in this case the sadness is caused by our learning here only the *negative* portion of the truth. Our air-castles are mournfully blown about by the rude winds of experience, which seem to moan out a requiem over things past and gone; while as yet we do not find the places once filled by these visionary buildings supplied by other, brighter, and more enduring ones. We see only the ruins, and have not yet seen the more glorious edifices that shall be; of which, indeed, those old and early structures were but harbingers and adumbrations. But hope, which is but faith in the future, —and spiritual faith, which is but hope stretched out to the embrace of the other and higher state of existence, — both assure us of love that shall satisfy our hearts, and of objects of love that shall fill in the sphere of our desire to help them and make them happy from ourselves. Partially, as facts of thought if not as facts of experience, we can already realize this delightful certainty, which only teaches us to live for heaven, and "so to run that we may obtain." These considerations impress upon us the necessity of another life as the complement of this; and are only instances which point us to trust in the compensations of that hereafter.

There is one more question suggested by our immediate subject, — How shall we recognize those who have gone before us, and whom we truly love? The consideration of this interesting inquiry we must defer, until we come to treat of the recognition of our children who have been removed in infancy into the other life.

From the review of the contents of this chapter we may see that two immutable truths confront us. These are perfectly consistent with each other, and with all other truths. One is, that in heaven there shall be a fulness of joy ; and the other is its consequent, that all those whom to remember and recognize and rejoin would enhance our or their felicity, will be remembered, recognized, and reunited. If there be any of those whom we may have loved here, but the recollection of whom may be there obliterated from our memories, we may rely upon it that they would not contribute to our happiness, nor should we to theirs. Earth, with its seemings, deceptions, and incongruities, will have faded away from the dwellers in that sphere of realities, and only the true, because the eternal, will survive.

# VI.

## MAN'S BOOK OF LIFE.

"And I saw the dead, small and great, stand before God; and the books were opened: and another book was opened, which is the book of life: and the dead were judged out of those things which were written in the books, according to their works." — REV. xx. 12.

AN ANALYSIS OF MEMORY. — ITS MARVELLOUS CHARACTERISTICS. — DO WE EVER FORGET? — THE SECRET OF REMEMBRANCE. — THE PHILOSOPHY OF MEMORY. — THE CONNECTION BETWEEN MAN'S MEMORY AND HIS REAL NATURE. — MAN'S TWO MEMORIES, THE EXTERNAL AND THE INTERNAL. — MAN'S MEMORY HIS "BOOK OF LIFE." — THE IMPOSSIBILITY OF SECRECY. — REWARDS ACCORDING TO WORKS. — THE GREAT ASSIZE. — COMPENSATIONS. — THE RECOLLECTIONS AND THE FORGETTINGS OF THE HEREAFTER. — HUMANITY'S HOPE IS REGENERATION. — THE DOUBLE MEANING OF FORGIVENESS OF SINS. — THE VALUE AND IMPORTANCE OF OUR PRESENT LIFE IN THE WORLD.

THE consideration of the foregoing properly introduces us to a more full and particular investigation of the nature of man's memory, as it refers to this and the future state of existence. This is the more necessary as we have spoken of one kind of memory that will forever endure, and of another kind of memory that may fade away, pale before the effulgence of spiritual light which must hereafter shine upon our souls.

From whatever point we commence to reflect upon our mental constitution, whether as to our power to *think* or our power to *will*, we are forced to confess, with the Psalmist, "I am fearfully and wonderfully made; marvellous are thy works, and that my soul knoweth right well." Of all our intellectual faculties, memory is certainly one of the most marvellous. By remembrance alone can we have any idea of duration. As by perception we are conscious of things that are present, so by recollection we are cognizant of things that are past. Things remembered are things that have been, and "we cannot conceive a thing to be past without conceiving some duration, more or less, between it and the present." Memory is also the sole proof to consciousness of our identity. We are consciously the same beings to-day that we were yesterday, because we remember the things which occurred yesterday. The destruction of memory would not, however, destroy our identity; for we should continue to be the same individuals, even though memory were obliterated. It is a certain fact that we do forget many things, yet our identity is not thereby rendered questionable. The fact of identity is one thing; the fact of our being conscious of that identity is quite another and different thing. The power of remembering proves our identity, but the proof is not the thing proved. Thus memory is dependent on identity, and is an evidence of it, but not contrariwise. Memory also is the foundation of experience, for experience is only the sum of our recollections. The wisdom which experience teaches is the previously observed, and now remembered, relation between certain causes and the results they produced.

This power of recalling to our consciousness the scenes we have beheld, the circumstances in which we have mingled, the trains of thought which we have indulged, the actions we have performed or submitted to, and the motives which impelled us to the performance of, or the submission to, those actions, is certainly a most wonderful power. It is capable of a development more extraordinary still, as is evinced by those persons who have been unusually endowed with this faculty, or who have most industriously cultivated it. Such rememberers of words as Cardinal Mezzofanti, or Sir William Jones, or Dr. Leyden, and others, or of facts such as Lord Macaulay, or Lord Brougham, and many others, afford us illustrations of what memory can be and do. The capabilities of this faculty appear to be limited only by the limitations of application and experience.

It is a question worthy serious consideration, whether in this life we can ever absolutely forget. Thousands of events which seem to have altogether faded away from the memory, or which are totally hidden behind more recent or more striking recollections, need only a suggestion, a small incident, a word, or a face, to recall them vividly to our consciousness. The recollection was there in the mind, although temporarily covered over, concealed from our consciousness, but not obliterated. Some persons can remember with distinctness events which occurred many years previously, although unable to recall circumstances of more recent occurrence. This peculiarity of memory is more especially observable after the persons have passed the middle term of life. Old age, sinking into a state of second childhood, recalls the recollections of the games of boyhood, and the tastes and dispositions of infancy. A thousand relatively insignificant remembrances flow back upon their consciousness, and the apparently altogether forgotten grows to be the most vividly perceived. This seems to confirm the idea that, though memory lapses, it never absolutely forgets. The experiences of persons undergoing the process of drowning, which have been remembered subsequently to their rescue, and described by Dr. Adam Clarke, and several others, tend in the same direction. Under such circumstances, memory appears to have been marvellously quickened, and their histories seem to have flashed in review before them, the recollections of many and long years being condensed into a moment of time. The impressions have been photographed upon the sensitive plate of memory, and they are probably ineffaceable.

While, however, there is a difference between various persons in power and coherence of memory and a second difference in the mode in which memory seems to operate in such various persons, there is also a remarkable difference in the memory of any one person at different times, or as to different subjects. Some memories are naturally more susceptible than others, or the impressions they receive appear to be invariably more vivid. In this there is only a similar disparity to what we may perceive in all other intellectual faculties. The perceptions of some may be more lively, and their conceptions may be more clear, than those of others; or some perceptions and some conceptions may be more lively in any one mind at some times than at others. The general rule, perhaps, may be asserted, that whatever most enlists the sympathies, or whatever most deeply involves the affections, is best remembered. This not only as to the absolute fact of such things being imprinted on the recollection, but also as to the relative and subordinate fact of our being conscious or cognizant of their presence in the memory. To say the same thing more simply, what most moves us we best remember. The emotion may be one of fear, of dislike, of remorse, or of love; but, in all cases, those events, which, as facts, most excited us at the time of their occurrence, remain as the most vivid recollections. Hence it is that cultivation of the memory is possible; for the sum of emotion produced by continuous reflection on a subject, which without that reflection we might forget, may be made to equal the sum of emotion which another subject excited at its first occurrence. The will of man is the inmost principle of his being. The affections or emotions of a man are, therefore, the inmost things of his life, the subtle waves of the ethereal and spiritual substances that constitute his soul. However various may be the thoughts into which they flow, the words by which they are described, or the actions by means of which they struggle into expression, these thrills of life which we call emotions are the primary consciousnesses of life. According to the depth, extent, and continuance of these emotions are the impressions produced upon our memories, and these impressions become, as it were, parts of our mental organisms. Memory, as a record, may thus be almost regarded as our real selves, such as the past has made us; and memory, as a consciousness, may be viewed as the revelation of our real natures to ourselves.

But this may seem obscure without a little dilation. Life is incessant activity. But the activity of life is of a twofold character. It is constituted of what we *do*, and of what we *receive*. What we *do* is our voluntary life of action; what we *receive* is our passive states of reception; or, more properly, it is the reflex action of life in us, produced by objects and causes external to ourselves. To illustrate these ideas:—A man beholds an object of charity, a suffering, needy family. He receives a host of impressions which they suggest, or call up within him. Thus far they produce in him a state of reflex action, or thus far he is receptive. He pities them. Here commences the direct and voluntary action in him. This emotion assumes form in his intellectual part as a thought of how he may relieve them. The emotion of pity prompts, and the thought to relieve directs the external action by which he does relieve them. The inmost ground of this external action was the emotion of pity. Whatever was the moral quality of this emotion, such was the true moral quality of both the thought and the external action. The moral quality of this emotion indicates the real moral quality or nature of the man.

All actions performed by man may be thus traced back from the act itself, through the thought which directed, to the emotion which prompted, both the thought and the deed. Between all three there is an intimate and exact correspondence. He acts for the accomplishment of a particular object, and according to a particular judgment. Even those actions which are ordinarily viewed as almost instinctive, and the least voluntary, have yet a motive, or an emotion, behind them, which may be traced by the person who has acted, and which, when clearly traced, will be clearly remembered by him. Indeed, the conscious remembrance will be either vivid or dim, confused or clear, as our perception of the motive or emotion was vivid or dim, confused or clear; shallow or profound, according to the superficiality or profoundness of the emotion itself.

It will be observed that we lay considerable stress on the distinction between memory as a fact, and the consciousness of that recollection. These two should not be confounded. Memory is no more dependent on consciousness of recollection than life is dependent on consciousness of living. In states of insensibility, produced, for example, by sound sleep, or injury to the brain, or a fit, we still live, albeit unconsciously; and in like manner memory may exist as a *fact*, while, as to our consciousness, recollection may have passed away. In such states memory sleeps, but is not dead.

In the illustration cited above, another fact may also be discerned. The man's act of charity, in reality, forms two distinct classes of impressions on his memory: one, of the persons whom he relieved, and the external circumstances under which he relieved them; and the other, of his own emotions and thoughts by which he was actuated and directed in relieving them. The latter is evidently more internal than the former, and belongs especially to the man; the former are but incidental circumstances associated with the act of charity. These incidental circumstances suggested the act to the impulses of his will, or they supplied them with an opportunity for action. The deed itself was only the outward expression of his emotional and intellectual life. The memory of the internal life is not only more interior, but it is also more permanent than the memory of the external circumstances. It is more permanent because it enters more deeply into our real natures. Our real natures, indeed, are changed and modified by the internal life we live. To practise charity as a habit is to render us charitable in our nature. To habituate one's self to selfishness will render one's nature selfish. What we feel modifies our will; what we think modifies our intellect; what we do modifies our external life; because our affectional nature is as the sum of our affections, our intellect is as the sum of our thoughts, and our external life is as the sum of our actions. But the real nature of the man accords far more with the character of his internal life of affection and thought, than with his external actions. All men have, and many men cherish, secret wishes and private thoughts, which, while they mould and modify their souls, are rarely exhibited by action or expressed by speech. We live an inner life which shrinks from the glare and exposure of day. This inner life may be good or it may be evil, nestling violets, or poisonous fungi, and humility may hide the one, and fear of consequences may conceal the other, but the fact of the inner life remains. The records of this inner life are graven in the inner memory. The inner memory of the man is far more operative upon his nature than is his external memory, and its results are more visible to his consciousness, and necessarily more permanent.

In our consciousness of memory, these internal recollections may be, and to some extent they must be, associated with our external memory, or our recollection of external events. Perhaps the reason of so many vague and shadowy recollections floating mistily before our consciousness, which like nebulous stars resist all our efforts to define them, and yet refuse to be dissipated, may be found in this, — the presence and permanence of the recollections of our internal memory, which yet are destitute of sufficient external associations by which to fix them as to locality and time. They are like bodiless ghosts of recollections restlessly roaming through the chambers of consciousness. We cannot clothe them, and we cannot drive them away. Their spiritual results continue, although the process by which they produced their results, as well as the circumstances under which they operated, are forgotten. However this may be, the fact remains of man's possessing "an *exterior* or corporeal memory proper to his bodily life, and an *interior* memory proper to his spirit." There is a universal language in which all men think, however different may be the natural languages in which they outwardly express their thoughts. The natural languages belong to the exterior memory, the universal language belongs to the interior memory which is common to all men. Hence is it that in the other life all spirits and angels can discern each others' thoughts and communicate their own.

It surely is not too extravagant a figure to describe man's double memory as the living pages of a written book. Man's memory of his own life is his "*Book of Life.*" All that he has done, thought, willed, is inscribed therein. The inscriptions are correct; for he himself is his own biographer. Neither fear of loss nor hope of gain can enable him to set down any of his actions in that book wrongly. Indeed, what he most strives to conceal from all others is most legibly written in his book of life. To conceal, he must remember; to conceal constantly, he must constantly remember; and to conceal effectually, the thing he strives to conceal can never leave his thoughts. In this living book which he *has*, and which also he *is*, the history of the whole man is written. It includes the histories of the three separate elements of his being; that of his will, his intellect, and his actions. As before said, the histories of the two former are not only inscribed in his memory, but also inscribed in his character. They form the limitation of his genius, the boundary lines of his dispositions; they make him what he is; and the more fully his consciousness is opened to the knowledge of himself, the more full will be the revelation to himself of his internal life, — of what he *is*. He may have performed actions which he is quite willing that all the world should behold, while the secret motives and hidden thoughts expressed in those actions he would not so willingly reveal.

Even while relying on the known inability of his fellows to discern all his true motives and thoughts in his performances, he cannot hide them from himself. Even those of which he is the least conscious still remain in his memory, and by reflection, or by other processes, he may become more largely conscious of them. If by neglect of reflection he does not become acquainted with them here, in the unveiling processes of the hereafter he will learn to "see himself as he is seen, and know himself as he is known."[1] From the tablets of his book of life he will learn his own history, and stand self-manifested to himself.

There is no such thing as complete secrecy as to the life of a man. He cannot, firstly, hide his life from himself. Even while here, this, to a great extent, is impossible. The voice of conscience will not be made dumb, and it is only by long and dire courses of evil that a man can deafen his soul to its reproaches. He cannot, secondly, hide his life from the angels. They can read the pages of his *book of life*, and they see him, often cowering behind the veils of hypocrisy and the disguises of custom, not as he would fain appear to be, but as he really is. "Thou God seest me" is, thirdly, the declaration of an unquestionable fact. "Whither shall I go from thy spirit? or whither shall I flee from thy presence? If I ascend up into heaven, thou art there; if I make

[1] 1 Cor. xiii. 12.

my bed in hell, behold, thou art there. If I take the wings of the morning and dwell in the uttermost parts of the sea; even there shall thy hand lead me, and thy right hand shall hold me. If I say, Surely the darkness shall cover me; even the night shall be light about me. Yea, the darkness hideth not from thee; but the night shineth as the day: darkness and light are both alike to thee."[1] He who trieth the reins, and understandeth all the secret thoughts of the children of men, unto whom all hearts are known, and from whom no thoughts can possibly be hid, He discerneth all our ways. At best we can only mask our real faces before those whose perceptions are limited by time and flesh, our competitors in the race and the struggle of physical existence, fellow-actors on this crowded and tumultuous scene; but with ourselves, the angels, and our God, all efforts at concealment are futile; "for in the other life the face will be the image of the mind."

If only partially effectual here, attempts at concealment will be altogether impossible in the other life. "The books shall be opened," and prominent among these, "*the book of life.*"[2] To prepare for the great assize which shall determine our final lots, the future state, and the companions we shall have made our own while in this lower earth-life, the memories of man, both his internal and external memories, shall be opened, and he shall

[1] Ps. cxxxix. 7-12. [2] Rev. xx. 12.

be judged according to the things written in those books. This judgment-day happens to all, and follows upon man's death. Not only do angels behold the book of life of the person undergoing judgment, but also the man himself. There is opened to his consciousness all that he is, and all that he has done, thought, and wished. The shams and affectations of time are melted with the mists that temporarily made him unconscious of his memories. Here on earth "we see through a glass, darkly; but then face to face: now I know in part; but then shall I know even as also I am known."[1] "Nothing that was covered here, but shall there be revealed; nothing that was hid here, but shall there be made known."[2] That which was here "spoken in the darkness shall there be heard in the light; and what was here spoken in the ear in closets shall there be revealed on the housetops."[3] The seeming and the mistaken shall be dissolved in the light of truth, and the realities of life shall there stand forth made manifest. The one talent of knowledge which has been hidden in the napkin shall be taken from the unprofitable servant, who shall be driven into outer darkness, and "unto him who hath (by having practised and improved upon his gift of wisdom and power) shall be given more abundantly; while from him who hath not shall be taken away even that which he seemeth to have."[4]

[1] 1 Cor. xiii. 12. [2] Matt. x. 26. [3] Luke xii. 3. [4] Matt. xxv. 28-30.

At the bar of this universal judgment-seat the accused will stand. The accusations are written in his own memories. The witnesses are within himself. "At the mouth of two or three witnesses shall every truth be established."[1] "At the mouth of two witnesses, or three witnesses, shall he that is worthy of death be put to death; but at the mouth of one witness he shall not be put to death."[2] The three witnesses who will give evidence are his will, his understanding, his life. According to their testimony will he be rewarded or condemned. His understanding may have been darkened by errors, and, cross-examined by truth, may give evidence against him; but if his heart and life are right in the sight of God, "at the mouth of one witness shall he not be put to death." His understanding may have been enlightened by Divine truth, he may have believed in the Gospel as a matter of intellectual acquiescence; but if his heart and life condemn him, these are the two witnesses whose evidence should be sufficient to condemn. "Their hands shall be first upon him to put him to death, and afterward the hands of all the people."[3] The first ministers of justice will be the very witnesses who have testified against him. Self-accused, self-condemned, self-destroyed, he will come under the mournful denunciation, "O Israel, thou hast destroyed thy-

[1] Matt. xviii. 16. [2] Deut. xvii. 6. [3] Deut. xvii. 7.

self,"[1] or under the operation of that eternal principle, "Evil shall slay the wicked."[2]

There is a principle of compensation at work even in this life. Though by no means so universal as some writers strive to represent, nor so reliable in its operation, yet sufficient to furnish an earthly shadowing forth of what in the spiritual world will be full and complete. Men are "rewarded according to their works" by their fellows. It is shown in the adoption of their inventions, in the diffusion of their thoughts, in the imitation of their modes, and in the effort to secure their results. I take not into account any pecuniary or social reward of the inventors or of the thinkers. While heartless ingratitude may be manifested to the men, the sincerest praise may be given by the acceptance of those ideas which they loved better than themselves. The heroes of the world have too often been the world's martyrs, and yet truth is never so sure of securing its triumph as when men hate it sufficiently to be induced to offer violent opposition thereto. In the widest sense, "the blood of the martyrs is the seed of the Church." The rack and the fagot, dungeons and torture, Gethsemane and Calvary, the world reserves for its sublimest teachers, and yet, despite them all, the Gospel has flourished, and truth finds the ever-increasing *few* who, loyal to truth, enforce its claims by their precepts, and illustrate its influence in their

1 Hosea xiii. 9. 2 Ps. xxxiv. 21.

lives. Torture may have weakened the force of the teacher, and death may have decimated the number of the taught, but they have only rejoiced in the certainty of their principles triumphing,—a certainty their sacrifices only rendered the more secure.

As human works approach a human standard of excellence, so they are adopted and valued by man. The standards change from age to age, and, since the coming of the Lord into the world, with an ever-increasing approximation to the perfect and the true. Not in vain has the "world swung adown the rattling grooves of change" for the last twenty centuries. But by man human productions are measured by an earthly standard. In the great judgment-day that comes to each individual who has passed out of the world, their works will be tested by a standard which is eternal and Divine. That standard of excellence will be the Word of God, the law revealed by God for our guidance. The Word will be opened; it is the great law-book, according to which man shall be judged concerning all those things written in his "book of life," his interior memory. Here, then, are all the necessary elements of a judgment:—God, the supreme judge; our own memories, the witnesses; angels and spirits, the attendant audience; the Bible, the great law; the recompense, "Well done, good and faithful servant, enter thou into the joy of thy Lord"; and the dread penalty, "Depart from me, ye cursed." Well may we exclaim with the prophet, "Who may abide the day of his coming? and who shall stand when he appeareth? for he is like a refiner's fire, and like fullers' soap: and he shall sit as a refiner and purifier of silver: and he shall purify the sons of Levi, and purge them as gold and silver, that they may offer unto the Lord an offering in righteousness."[1] Or with the Apostle, "For other foundation can no man lay than that is laid, which is Jesus Christ. Now if any man build upon this foundation gold, silver, precious stones, wood, hay, stubble; every man's work shall be made manifest: for the day shall declare it, because it shall be revealed by fire; and the fire shall try every man's work of what sort it is. If any man's work abide which he hath built thereupon, he shall receive a reward. If any man's work shall be burned, he shall suffer loss: but he himself shall be saved, yet so as by fire."[1]

Judgment being completed by the man becoming altogether *outwardly* what he is *inwardly*, his interior memory will become his only memory. The recollection of truth which dwelt in his exterior memory because acquired, but which never entered into his interior memory because not loved and practised, will be closed up, taken from him, as we learn in the parable of the talents; so that to his evil shall be added falsity, or, rather, the

[1] Mal. iii. 2, 3. [2] 1 Cor. iii. 11-15.

evils of his will shall assume their corresponding form of falsity in his understanding. Just as the Divine Love and Wisdom are one in God, so Goodness and Truth are one and the same thing in their absolute reality. They appear to be different things, because the unity is viewed by two different faculties. The *will*-side of truth is goodness; the *understanding*-side of goodness is truth. Every good rationally perceived is a truth; and every truth felt in the will is a good. Those who are in goodness shall receive truth, or shall be enabled to rationally perceive and apprehend the good that they love; and, contrariwise, those who are in evil must sink into falsities. The evil and the false are similarly co-related, as are goodness and truth. The *will*-side of falsity is evil, and the *understanding*-side of evil is falsity. He that is filthy shall become altogether filthy, and he that is righteous shall be "clothed with white robes." The man, both as an angel and a demon, must become homogeneous; the angel will no longer have to cope with errors, or to struggle with ignorance, — the love of the good will be robed in its appropriate apprehension of truth; and the demon will have wholly given himself up to a lie, and become as perverted in perception as corrupt in heart. From both the exterior memory will be sunk out of sight, and the interior memory will alone remain. On this great principle, then, will be determined the recollections and the forgettings of the hereafter.

This does not contradict the previous assertion of distinctions and differences both in heaven or hell. The demons as well as the angels are in various degrees, and possess various specialties. Individuality is preserved, and preserved, indeed, the more thoroughly, by each becoming manifestly, externally as well as internally, *what he really is.*

There are, however, questions of vast practical importance that grow out of the foregoing considerations. It may be said that this seems to be rather the revelation of despair than a gospel of hope to the sinner. "Weighed in the balances, and found wanting," would have to be the dread verdict found against every child of Adam. Where then is there hope?

The only hope for humanity is contained in the Gospel injunction to become "new creatures." The old evils of the "old man" must be purged away by the operations of God's Spirit in the soul. This purgation is of a double kind. It is, first, from man's consciousness, the blessed consequence of sincere and contrite repentance; and, secondly, from man's inmost and real being, by a life of holiness. The first removal of sins from our consciousness is depicted in the consolatory words of the Lord, "Son, be of good cheer; thy sins be forgiven thee"; [1] and the final removal of evil from our being is intimated in the words, "Sin

[1] Matt. ix. 2.

no more, lest a worse thing come upon thee."[1] There are relapses into sin, and there are more complete triumphs over sin; the middle term of both states is the first forgiveness of sin, or its removal from the consciousness. Because there are two degrees of remission of sins, there are two classes of passages in the Word of God, — the one avowing the irrevocable promise of forgiveness as the result of repentance, and the other indicating the necessity of personal victory, growing in grace, and being "nearer unto salvation than when we believed."[2] Referring to both, that most magnificent exhortation of the Prophet is given to us, "Wash you, make you clean; put away the evil of your doings from before mine eyes; cease to do evil; learn to do well; seek judgment, relieve the oppressed, judge the fatherless, plead for the widow. Come now, and let us reason together, saith the Lord: though your sins be as scarlet, they shall be white as snow; though they be red like crimson, they shall be as wool. If ye be willing and obedient, ye shall eat the good of the land."[3] The forgiveness that follows repentance is the Christian life *begun;* the fuller eradication of the very dispositions that previously led us to sin is the Christian life made *perfect.* It is the confirmation within us of the first remission, as is sublimely intimated in the epistle, "Whoso keepeth his word, in him verily is the love of God per-

[1] John v. 14. [2] Rom. xiii. 11. [3] Isa. i. 16-19.

fected: hereby we know we are in him";[1] for as the Apostle also instructs us, "*If we walk in the light, even as he is in the light*, [then] we have fellowship one with another, and [then] the blood of Jesus Christ cleanseth from all sin. . . . . If we confess our sins, he is faithful and just to forgive us our sins, and [further] *to cleanse us from all unrighteousness*."[2] By the grace and mercy of the Lord Jesus Christ, therefore, we can in verity become "*new creatures;* old things shall pass away, and all things become new."[3] Herein is the true power and glorious operation of regeneration, so that in the judgment we may stand and be accepted of Him. Christ will have "blotted out our transgressions for his own sake, and will not remember our sins."[4] He will have turned his "hand upon us, and have purged away our dross, and have taken away all our tin."[5] Troubled as we have been, and still are, by our old heart, and bewildered by the musings of our old spirit, our life's prayer should be, "Create in me a clean heart, and renew a right spirit within me."[6]

As regeneration is a great fact in human experience, so it, too, will be inscribed on the tablets of our "book of life," and the lustre of this new inscription will eclipse and efface the sins which the "old man" committed, and the evils which the "old man" desired. It will create a

[1] 1 John ii. 5.
[2] 1 John i. 7.
[3] 2 Cor. v. 17.
[4] Isa. xliii. 25.
[5] Isa. i. 25.
[6] Ps. li. 10.

new will, and a new internal memory, and the old memory and its records will be hidden out of sight.

But alas for the unregenerate dead! As we live, so we die; and as we die, so shall we live hereafter. We cannot put back the hands on the broad dial-plate of existence. "The filthy shall be filthy still; the unjust shall be unjust still; the righteous and the holy shall be righteous and holy still."[1] The allotted term for our preparation will be completed, and eternity shall only seal the balances of time. On the everlasting tablets of their memories men will have written the records of their lives. The secret wishes that they dared not whisper are all there. All there the dark and evil thoughts that wound themselves through the labyrinth of their minds. The hidden acts by which they sought to realize their wish, and express their thought, are all there. All there, too, in a state where secrecy and solitude have no power, where the brand burned in by the effort to conceal it here, shall stand livid, conspicuous, ineffaceable. There, too, graven on imperishable tablets, will be the kind charities, the tender affections, the earnest efforts to help and bless others, which the good may have made. Hypocrisy cannot hide those, and these modesty cannot veil.

Now, too, in this life, are the possibilities of reformation, and the opportunities for repentance.

[1] Rev. xxii. 11.

Happy they who, hearing the "Mene, Mene, Tekel, Upharsin," determine to change. Woe to them against whom the "Mene, Tekel," is pronounced as the dread summing up of their account, the final sentence of their misery and doom!

# VII.

## INFANTS IN HEAVEN.

"It is not the will of your Father who is in the heavens, that one of these little ones should perish." — MATT. xviii. 14.

GOD'S LOVE TO LITTLE CHILDREN. — THE MOTHER'S LOVE. — THE SANCTITY OF PATERNITY. — GOD'S MERCY MANIFESTED IN ITS PERMISSION. — THE SPIRITUAL USES OF PATERNITY. — JOY IN HEAVEN OVER THE BIRTH OF OUR LITTLE ONES. — DEATH OF CHILDREN. — ALL WHO DIE IN INFANCY ETERNALLY SAVED. — HEREDITARY EVIL AND ACTUAL SIN. — THE EPITAPHS OF INFANTS. — MOURNING FOR BABES THAT HAVE DIED. — WHY DO CHILDREN DIE? — RECOGNITION OF OUR CHILDREN IN THE OTHER LIFE. — WILL THEY FOREVER REMAIN INFANTS? — GROWTH IN HEAVENLY WISDOM AND GOODNESS. — ANGELS THE TUTORS OF OUR ANGELIC BABES. — CONCLUSIONS ON THE TOPIC. — GENERAL PRACTICAL LESSON OF THE WHOLE WORK.

OD is a dear and loving friend of little children. In His watchful and tender providence He has so ordered it that the cradle of incipient manhood should be surrounded with an atmosphere of love. Offsprings and effigies of love, love receives, welcomes, tends, and toils for the little ones intrusted to human care. The maternal instinct, as it has been termed, is certainly one of the strongest feelings implanted in all animals. Human mothers share this feeling in common with all animals, and in them it is also ennobled by being *humanized*, — that is, filled with a deeper tenderness, prolonged during ampler periods, elevated by spiritual anxieties, and purified by unselfish care. No delight can equal that of the young mother as she clasps for the first time "her miracle" to the sanctuary of her love, and the font of its sustenance, — her bosom. Her delight is enhanced by the consideration that her babe is an immortal being, the offspring of her life, but destined to an existence as eternal as her own. She has been one of the instruments used by God for the fashioning of an imperishable structure, and in its babyhood the little one seems all her own. It draws the sustentation of its life from her heart as it drew its life thence. She is its parent and its sustainer. God evinces His love for humanity in having prepared the mother's body to bear and the mother's devotion to welcome the babe. He has exquisitely chosen the known tenderness of a mother's love to lend force to His inspired description of His own love for mankind, "Can a woman forget her sucking child, that she should not have compassion on the son of her womb? yea, they may forget, yet will I not forget thee."[1]

But a human father shares this affection, and an additional source of love to welcome the child is furnished in the fond impulses of his heart. Though the feeling of the father toward the little one must necessarily be different in kind and degree from

[1] Isa. xlix. 15.

that experienced by the mother, yet it will not yield in strength, although, perhaps, surpassed in tenderness. When infancy begins to take tottering and feeble steps, and strives to break out into half-articulated words, the mother's treasure becomes as much the man's. To labor for its wants, and to strive to form its little and eager mind, — the memory of its smiles, and the lingering happiness of its kiss, become new cheerers of existence, and fresh incentives to effort. "When I come home," grows to be a sweeter thought, from the hope of meeting the little ones that shall cluster about his knees, cling to his neck, and call him "Father." In permitting to man this sacred and solemn name, God has portrayed in every family circle the relationship which exists between His universal children and Himself. Paternal love is the mirror in which we may see the reflection of His Divine love for us; for language has no sublimer appellation of the Deity than "OUR FATHER." In supplying our little ones with a representative of Himself, God thereby manifests how truly He loves His little lambs.

Babes are surrounded with a still wider circle of lovers. Brothers and sisters, relatives and friends, are ready to welcome it, and who can tell what influences of joy are brought to bear upon the little new-comer by the thrilling heart-throbs and lingering kisses that strong men, and tender women, and delighted children feel toward, and press upon, the pink lips and round white cheeks of the baby? Incapable of estimating their worth or of expressing its appreciation, yet so far as it is conscious at all the infant must derive happiness from such sources. Loving hearts are blessings to the babe, and none the less because it may be unconscious of their presence and ignorant of their tenderness.

God also manifests His love toward His creatures by confiding to their care these helpless pledges of human affection. If by some strange, and to us inconceivable process, children should start into life full-grown, wholly independent of our anxieties, how much of the delight of life, as well as the uses of life, would thereby vanish away! Life has no more efficient schoolmaster for training us in unselfishness, devotion, and kindness than our having to provide for the wants, and being permitted to foster and reciprocate the attachments, of our offspring. The fondness that exists between friends is based on sympathy, the giving and receiving intellectual and emotional gratification. The love that exists between married partners is necessarily founded in reciprocal attachment, the desire of giving and receiving — and too often of receiving rather than giving — mutual aid, mutual comfort, mutual delight. In both relations we look for, and are right in looking for, a *return* of our devotion, — at least, the consciousness in them of the self-sacrifice we make, and a return in tenderness toward ourselves for the tenderness we exhibit. There is something of selfishness underlying the purest friendship, or conjugal fondness, which we can feel; but the love of infants is the most unselfish feeling of our nature. From them we can hope for no immediate return. They may pass away from this state of being long before they have learned to recognize our features, our voice, or our touch. We cannot hope in many cases that the little ones will repay back even love for love. Even with the worst men and women this love is therefore the most disinterested, — the most like God's love.

Children are the most helpless of beings, and we love them because we can help them; they are the most dependent, and we toil for them the most willingly. The love of children brings us nearer to innocence; nearer to Paradise, the state of innocence; nearer to God, the absolutely holy and pure.

Conjugal love is one of the sublimest affections and richest privileges permitted to man, the pure and holy love of the husband for the wife, and of the wife for her husband. Nothing, however, so strongly cements this marriage union between two sympathizing souls as the birth of children. Not only do the little ones bring love for themselves as they come into the world, but they bring deeper and holier love, a richer and ampler joy, a closer and sweeter union, a wider and stronger peace, to the lives of their parents. They are the blossoms on the tree of human marriage, and a babe renders its parents more thoroughly one in the common interest which they acquire by their common possession of it. Wisely and well spoke the Psalmist in asserting, "Lo, children are an heritage from the Lord: and the fruit of the womb is his reward. As arrows in the hand of the mighty, so are the children of youth. Happy is the man that hath his quiver full of them."[1] "Thy children shall be as olive-plants round about thy table. Behold, that thus shall the man be blessed who feareth the Lord."[2] If in the present states of human existence these blessings are not altogether realized by the possession of families, it is only an evidence of disorder. It is only because of the greatness of the joy which having children in states of order would procure, that greatness of misery results so often from having families in states of disorder. From the loftiest height we experience the severest fall. The joy of the blessing, and the pain of its perversion, are equal and contrary. Through the same wide-open avenue along which joy might have flowed in upon us, sorrow also comes, and the intensity of the sorrow is only the proof of how deep should have been the joy.

The surest evidence of the unselfing operation of children on married partners is to be found in the merely selfish reasons which the childless urge for being satisfied with their lot. They are spared pain, care, anxiety, disappointment, many burdens,

[1] Ps. cxxvii. 3-5. [2] Ps. cxxviii. 3, 4.

and much possible disappointment. True; and well is it for them if some other beings than themselves are the better for their preservation from the cares and troubles of parentage.

The birth of a child is, however, provocative of more than human joy. According to the words of the Lord, "there is joy in heaven over every sinner that repenteth": human joy, when pure and holy, reaches beyond the narrow limits of our own private circles. The earth is the seminary of heaven. God's purpose concerning every man is, that he shall become an angel in heaven. It is only by dint of doing despite to the mercy and Spirit of God, that man can frustrate the Divine purpose. Against the possibility of man's final loss are leagued God, His angels, His purposes, the Redemption which He came to effect, and the operations of His Spirit which He continually bestows. Only the comparative omnipotence of the human *will* can prevent man's salvation. The angels know when we repent, the angels must also know when we are born. They must know when we are born, also, because every human child has guardian angels, — "their angels," as the Lord beautifully described them, to which reference was made in the second chapter of this work. If the angels rejoice at another human being becoming, by repentance, potentially "an inheritor of the kingdom of heaven," equally must they rejoice at the accession to existence of a new living creature, who is also potentially "an heir of glory, and a co-heir with Jesus Christ." The angels rejoice over the repenting sinner, because he has entered upon the initiative process by which he may become one of themselves. This were charity, large enough to be angelic. But as they are "all ministering spirits, sent forth to minister unto those who shall be the heirs of salvation,"[1] they rejoice to have a new patient upon whom to operate, a new object of their love, a new subject to whom to offer their tender uses. And so, too, with our children. God intends them for heaven, and this merciful design they can realize, if they so determine. Therefore do the angels love them much. They form also subjects for angelic ministrations, and the ever-burning flame of angelic love desires an ever-increasing activity, whereby they may manifest it. Therefore do the angels love them the more. The chorus of gladness that wells forth from the hearts of the parents is caught up by the angelic choirs, and its echoes are resounded in heaven. The brotherhood and sisterhood of the skies hail the advent of the little stranger, who is as much a new-comer into their world as into ours. We welcome it from love, and their love for it surpasses and exceeds our own. The multitude of the heavenly host, who sang their song of praise and adoration at the birth of the Saviour,[2] were only more rapturous, and their song was only set in more lofty strains than

[1] Heb. i. 14. [2] Luke ii. 13, 14.

the song that heralds in the advent of every child which is born.

Yet children die! It is estimated that one third of the human race passes away from the world while they are yet infants. Not more than one half live to attain manhood or womanhood.

"There is no flock, however watched and tended,
But one dead lamb is there;
There is no fireside, howsoe'er defended,
But has one vacant chair.

"The air is full of farewells to the dying,
And mournings for the dead;
The heart of Rachel for her children crying,
Will not be comforted!"

The little ones, who are like "rainbows on our dark of life," too often seem as

"those
Who come with pledge and promise not to stay";

and just as the soul has learned to feel all the sweet intoxication of their presence, —

"In Death's face hers flashed up and smiled,
As smile the young flowers in their prime
I' the face of their gray murderer Time,
And Death for true love kissed our child."

Heart-bruised, vacant, and yearning, and weary, what shall we say of the little ones who have departed? I know nothing more beautiful and true than those sweet words of Gerald Massey: —

"Through Childhood's morning land serene,
She walked betwixt us twain, like Love;
While, in a robe of light above,
Her better Angel walked unseen,

"Till Life's highway broke bleak and wild;
Then, lest her starry garments trail
In mire, heart bleed, and courage fail,
The Angel's arms caught up the child."

We must say of them, that God needed them for His kingdom, and He, who lent them to us for a little while, hath recalled them to Himself.

Never was a doctrine taught that is more abhorrent to the heart and intellect of man, than that some little children are everlastingly lost. Fatuity and falsehood never culminated into a more monstrous form than this. It is only calculated to make man fear God as a ruthlessly partial God, and an inexorable tyrant. No amount of reasoning can overcome the invincible repugnance such a doctrine must excite in the least susceptible. It is the frightful progeny of mercilessness and error, spawned by callous hearts in an age of iron cruelty and densest darkness. The moral tendency of such a doctrine is only to partiality the most iniquitous, and to wanton vindictiveness. To assert that God has reprobated some to everlasting perdition, and no matter how young they may be when they enter into eternity, everlasting perdition must still be their lot, is the sufficient confutation of the whole theory of election. It would robe the Deity in the lurid vestments of a demon, and the worship of such a being would degenerate into horror and dread.

In the Word of God, children are named as

types of innocence, holiness, and purity. "At the same time came the disciples unto Jesus, saying, Who is greatest in the kingdom of heaven? And Jesus called a little child unto him, and set him in the midst of them, and said, Verily I say unto you, Except ye be converted, and become as little children, ye shall not enter into the kingdom of heaven."[1] More explicitly still than even by this implication, did He declare, "Suffer the little ones to come unto me, and forbid them not; *for of such is the kingdom of heaven.*"[2] Not only must children in these passages be regarded as the types of the "babes in Christ," the true "babes and sucklings out of whose mouths God has perfected praise";[3] the symbols of the "little flock," who were exhorted not to fear, because it was "the Father's good pleasure to give them the kingdom";[4] but we must understand these passages to be declaratory of an actual fact in relation to the children themselves, — "Of such is the kingdom of heaven." Babes are God's little ones, and when He calls them away from earth He gathers them to Himself.

The contrary opinion has originated in a failure, which has been only too prevalent, to perceive an important distinction. All who come into the world are infected with the moral virus of hereditary evil; but this hereditary evil, sometimes mis-

1 Matt. xviii. 1-3.
2 Matt. xix. 14.
3 Matt. xxi. 16.
4 Luke xii. 32.

named "original sin," does not become actual *sin*, until the child attains such an age as to knowingly and wilfully commit sin. Under the curse is every man's child, because receiving this fearful entail of hereditary predisposition to evil; but no such child can be a *sinner*, until by actual and conscious indulgence he makes his involuntary hereditament *his own*, by willing and doing evil. "Sin is the transgression of the law," and till the law is known, it cannot be transgressed. Only *sinners*, the voluntary transgressors of the law, are amenable to the penalties attached to transgression. However hereditarily evil, yet children are not sinners, and cannot therefore be condemned. The great and just law of condemnation is thus emphatically set forth in the sacred Scriptures: "The soul that sinneth, it shall die. The son shall not bear the iniquity of the father, neither shall the father bear the iniquity of the son: the righteousness of the righteous shall be upon him, and the wickedness of the wicked shall be upon him."[1] Yet in the frightful entail upon the children of predispositions to evil, fearfully increased by the indulgences of the parents, is the warning of the Lord fulfilled; He "visiteth the sins of the fathers upon the children unto the third and fourth generation of them that hate him."[2] In this life does the latter sentence receive its dread execution; but in the next life, a human being stands or falls, according to

[1] Ezek. xviii. 20. [2] Exod. xx. 5.

the deeds of his own life, as is conclusively shown in the whole of the eighteenth chapter of Ezekiel. However hereditarily evil, therefore, a child who dies in its infancy is saved. Their evils have never been made sins in them by indulgence. Their voluntary life is a blank page. They are types of the innocence of wisdom, because they are absolutely in the innocence of ignorance; and "of such is the kingdom of heaven."

The God-written testimonies implanted in the deep heart-wisdom of loving parents who have lost their little ones, add only confirmation to this comfort-inspiring view. The epitaphs inscribed on the little headstones, that coldly mark the spot where their "earthly house of this tabernacle" lies dissolving away, touchingly express the words of consolation which God's good Spirit whispers to the souls of the bereaved ones. Their children are in heaven, taken by the angels home to God. Speaking in the solemn heart-thoughts of the sorrowing, the Spirit only bears witness to the truth previously revealed in the Bible, — "Of such is the kingdom of heaven."

We need not too profoundly mourn when our children are removed, or, rather, however much we mourn our own loss, the bright certainty of their gain ought to lift us out of selfish grief. We can follow them in thought into their Father's mansions on high. To have a child in heaven, is only to have our own hearts bound about with a golden cord that is gently drawing our steps upwards, heavenwards, homewards. It is only an inducement the more for us to "run the race," and pursue the path of our pilgrimage, that we may rejoin them where loving hearts shall know no parting, and kindred souls shall dwell together forever. Angel fingers beckon us onward, angel voices encourage us in the silent hours of trial and gloom, angel smiles cheer us in the dark valley, and it is only all the sweeter to remember that some of them may be the little ones whom we have loved and given up to God. "I am a blossomless tree!" sinks sadly into the loving heart that feels how much it has lost when its babe was taken from her arms: "I am the mother of an angel!" may dissipate the darkness and wipe away the tears, mingle a smile with the weeping, pour balm into the gaping wound, and reveal the silver lining of the frowning cloud.

But doubt comes again with its questions. Why do not all die in infancy, if to die then is so blessed and certain gain? The world's work must go on, and some — a sufficient number — must remain to do it. Why are not those alone taken, whom the Lord foreknows will prove wicked and be lost? Here we must cover our lips, and the heart must enjoin "TRUST" on the intellect. Bad men may have good children, who may derive from their parents such an hereditary intellectual character as shall fit them to do work in the world which none others would be so well able to accomplish, and who could not have been born into the world at all had it not been for the preservation of their parents. A generation of angels, too, may spring from an ancestry that was evil. We are, however, met here by the vast subject of the intellectual adaptation of individuals to be the agents of the Divine Providence in the development of the human race, and the promotion of its progress. But even speculation can here only go haltingly, and we are compelled to confide in the thought, that in the final summing up of "God in account with His children," it will be seen that the lesser evil has been permitted in order to secure the greater good; and that, in view of the immensity of that good, the evil will be no more than spots on the sun of its brightness. Yet, why should there be spots on the sun at all? The truth must be confessed, — the whole subject only presents us with an additional view of the many-sided problem of the permission of evil. This life only furnishes us with one term of the problem, we must wait till the next state of existence supplies us with the second term. This is but true wisdom after all; for to break our hearts in striving in the darkness is only the dictate of folly. We must wait for the light, rejoicing in the certainty that the day will dawn upon this, and many other problems, at present insoluble, when the shadows of our earth-life are lifted. It is at least a merciful providence that the vast majority of those who die in infancy are physically the least fitted to remain; though even to this there seem some exceptions, so far as our human wisdom extends, which, however, extends so small a distance after all. Where it has pleased the Divine Mercy to reveal so little, dogmatism would only be an evidence of temerity. We believe and trust.

There are other questions which we must desire to ask, and to which, from Scriptural and rational sources, some sort of a reply may be gained. Shall we be able to recognize our children on the other side? Will they remain children in the other life forever?

The mode of recognition in the other life appears to be altogether of a different nature from that we are acquainted with here. *Here* we recognize our friends only from external signs, and our mutual recognitions are confirmed by interchanges of recollections. *There*, perception, and consequently recognition, is of a spiritual or interior character. An illustration of this idea is furnished in the narrative of the Transfiguration. The three disciples were able to know the heavenly beings who ministered unto the Lord. "Lord, it is good," said Peter, "for us to be here: if thou wilt, let us make here three tabernacles; one for thee, and one for Moses, and one for Elias."[1] Although the Apostles could not, of course, have previously known

[1] Matt. xvii. 4.

these two holy prophets, and, therefore, could not have *recognized* them, yet, without any intimation as to who they were, they obtained an inward perception as to their individuality. They knew them. The Lord also furnishes us with a further illustration of this remarkable fact in the parable of the rich man and Lazarus. Not only is the rich man described as recognizing Lazarus, whom he had known on earth, but also he appeared to know Abraham, whom he had never seen. Whatever may be the changes which residence in the spiritual world will effect in the personal appearance of those who precede us, the desire to be with them will produce their presence, and that same similarity of state, from which proceeded the spiritual desire, will enable us to know them.

The second question, whether infants will forever remain infants, is, perhaps, more difficult of solution. The difference between a child and an adult, viewed as to their spiritual natures, consists solely in the ignorance and undeveloped nature of the infant, and in the superior knowledge and wisdom of the adult. We cannot presume that children who enter into the other life will forever remain ignorant, or childish in the sense of being ignorant, and incapable of rational thought. As God is essentially Love and Wisdom, and as the angels receive more fully of the Divine life than man, so their reception of the Divine life must cause an increase of the love and wisdom which they derive from God. They become more like God by knowing more of His truth, and partaking of more of His goodness. As they will forever increasingly receive of the Divine gifts, so they will forever increase in wisdom and goodness, become more and more fully men, "images and likenesses of God." This universal principle cannot surely be affected by the circumstance of the age, or the state of spiritual development of the individual angel at the period when he first enters upon his angelic condition. Compared with that future development, the wisest man on earth is but as a child, only a little larger than his fellows. Progress is, therefore, as much the destiny of the child-angel as of the angel who attained manhood before quitting this mortal sphere. This progress will be in the perception of wisdom and the reception of love from the Lord. The true idea of spiritual maturity is spiritual fulness; and as the child-angel will increasingly receive of this fulness, so he must increasingly become matured in the kingdom of heaven. But it is also true that an angel is homogeneous; that is, his exterior appearance of brightness, beauty, and glory is exactly representative of his inner and real state; and, therefore, as the child-angel becomes wiser he becomes brighter, as he grows more loving he grows more beautiful, he is the more glorious as he receives of the holiness which is the glory of God, and he appears more manlike as he becomes more Godlike, for Jesus is the true pattern of a man. There seems, then, every presumption in favor of the spiritual *form* of the child-angel attaining its proper dimensions, or of its growing into the appearance of manhood. There may be, and doubtless is, some difference which will everlastingly remain between those angels who departed from their earth-life during their infancy and those who attained maturity before their departure; but it is most reasonable to think that such differences will consist in the special relation their states sustain to those of others, and the angelic uses to which they are thereby peculiarly adapted, rather than in their eternal retention of an infantile size or form.

While every presumption is in favor of their growth, there is no rational necessity for the contrary opinion. It is no more necessary that they should retain their size, than that they should retain their individual appearances of form or features. They may have been relatively coarse or ugly, or malformed or even deformed, and of course these things are inconsistent with heavenly beauty and perfection, — inconsistent, moreover, with the intrinsic beauty of their souls. Some of the loveliest souls I have known were burdened with a heritage of physical deformity. Stunted growth, curved spines, withered limbs, may be the temporary appanages of the pure and loving, who live a life of martyrdom here, and are preparing for a martyr's crown hereafter; but when enfranchised from the slavery of flesh, and delivered from the dungeons of deformity, the pure spirit shall be bright and beautiful as it is really humble and good. There exists no reason why the size of the body or its shape should inexorably mould the spirit into the same form. This is not even necessary for purposes of recognition, as we have before shown; and that they might be recognized, would furnish the only exterior grounds of necessity. The argument is equally apposite and forcible in the case of children.

Nor is there any Scriptural evidence in support of the contrary opinion. Cherubs and baby-angels are conceptions of old painters, but nowhere justified in the Word of God. Even though justified as to the fact that there had been child-angels, still the Bible supplies no proof of such continuing to be children in size and appearance forever. No: it is more reasonable to presume that they will mature in form as in wisdom and in holiness, attaining a sublime manhood of appearance as well as of perception and of love. Angels are all childlike because innocent; an infant is the type of angels because of its innocence; but though childlike they are not *childish* in form of appearance, or in grasp of intellect, or in fervor of love. The poet Longfellow has caught what seems to us the true idea, and has exquisitely depicted it in his poem entitled "Resignation."

"There is no death! What seems so is transition:
This life of mortal breath
Is but a suburb of that life elysian,
Whose portal we call death!

"She is not dead, the child of our affection,
But gone unto that school
Where she no longer needs our poor protection,
And Christ himself doth rule.

"In that great cloister's stillness and seclusion,
By angel guardians led;
Safe from temptation, safe from sin's pollution,
She lives, whom we call dead.

"Not as a child shall we again behold her;
For when with rapture wild,
In our embraces we again enfold her,
She will not be a child:

"But a fair maiden in her Father's mansion,
Clothed with celestial grace,
And beautiful with all the soul's expansion,
Shall we behold her face!"

It is easy to conceive of what loving labor it must be to the angels to train and develop the infant minds intrusted to their care. It is evidently a mistake to suppose that immediately on entrance into heaven the child should comprehend all things. It is contrary to all we know of the laws of mind. Though amplified in their power, and quickened in their perceptions after the separation has taken place between their spirits and their bodies, yet from the modes in which mind operates *here*, we may see at least an indication of how mind will operate *there*. It may be more rapid in its growth, but the idea of growth is inextricably involved in our conception of the wisdom of angels. The labor of acquisition is *here* toilsome and painful; *there* it shall become an ever-increasing source of bliss. Our progress *here* is at best but slow and wearisome; *there* it will be rapid and delightful. *Here* the subjects that mostly occupy us are of the earth, earthy; *there* they will be Godlike and heavenly. *Here* we dare not place implicit confidence in any teacher, for in all there is not only deficiency, but also defect; *there*, however relatively deficient in their wisdom the angels may be, yet they will mingle no falsehood with their truths, no errors with their instructions. But in both states there must exist this double similarity; — becoming wise is a *process*, and, further, that in this process God will make use of intelligent instrumentalities.

Only infinite capacity can possess infinite wisdom. Finite capacities, however enlarged, must be finite, in two respects, — as to the extent and range of wisdom they receive, and also as to the necessity of their advancing from one perception to another by gradations. Only to the Absolutely Wise is there neither to-day, yesterday, nor to-morrow in His wisdom. Time adds nothing to His eternity, and experience nothing to His knowledge. It is and must be thus with God only. The law which obtains in all others is the law of progress. Angels grow wiser by experience, and this necessitates an increase in wisdom that is *gradual*, and this gradual increase is the *process* above referred to. In common with all angels, the child who is taken to heaven will increase in wisdom, and this from state to state. "Line upon line, precept upon precept," is as much the God-declared law of angelic improvement, as it is the necessary law of human progress. In the Divine Being alone is Wisdom absolute: compared with this, the knowledge attained unto by angels will eternally be relative, yet it will hold the relation of more or less: least when they first enter upon their heavenly state, but continually growing more and more as they continue to abide there. How rapid is their progress none can say; but, rapid as it may be, it is simply irrational to believe that as soon as a child becomes altogether an inhabitant of the spiritual world he springs by a momentaneous impulse into all the wisdom of the angels, and into the comprehension of all the science of the skies.

There must also be this further similarity between both states of existence; God will make use of intelligent instrumentalities for the instruction of heavenly neophytes. All truth originates in God, but truth may flow down from God either by an immediate or a mediate way, or it may reach us by both modes. It does reach us by both modes during our existence here; but what we learn from others far surpasses in amount what we learn by meditation, or that wisdom which reaches us by an internal method. It is no denial of God's being the sole original source of all wisdom, for us to receive knowledge through the mediumship of teachers; nor is it at all derogatory to the majesty of the Divine Providence that He should make use of instrumentalities. Indeed, the communication of truth is one of the instrumentalities God employs for enhancing the delight of wisdom in His children; for truth seems never so delightful to its possessor as it does while he makes an effort to communicate it. The love of truth and the love of communicating truth cannot be separated; and we may safely conclude that as the state of the neophyte angel is one of progress, and therefore of reception, so the wisdom of the angels will impart new joy to them because of their endeavor to communicate their gift to the truth-thirsting souls of those less wise than they. While, consequently, the new-comers will "see light in God's light," or derive wisdom immediately from the inspiration of God, yet will they also receive instructions from heavenly instruments, and thus derive wisdom from God *mediately* as well as *immediately*. "Kings shall be their nursing fathers, and queens their nursing mothers," in order that they may be more fully the children of the great All-Father by "receiving everlastingly of His fulness." Their brothers, the angels, are their tutors; heaven is their sublime academy, and God the great master from whom all their wisdom flows.

To conclude, then, children are the love-blossoms on the tree of human life. They are given by a God of love, in love to man, committed by the Divine love, to the bosom of our love. When He sees best for them to depart from our human arms they are received by welcoming angels, who guide their ascending footsteps up to God. We may treasure our fond memories of them in our hearts, we may hope to meet and know them in the hereafter. Death has no real sting, for it reaches not to them. The grave has gained no real victory, for our separation from them is only a thing which a few weeks may, and a few years must, terminate. "It is better to have loved and lost than never to have loved at all"; besides, our departed children are not lost. They will not come back to us, but we shall go to them; and if we are like them in the innocence of our souls, in our love to God, and in our capacities of use, we shall dwell with them for ever and ever. "Christ hath abolished death" in this high sense, and thus has brought "life and immortality to light by the Gospel." And even though our states may be dissimilar to those of our departed dear ones, and separation thence result, still our grateful and adoring spirits, penetrated with submission to the Divine wisdom, and wrought into unity with the Divine will, shall still rejoice in the thought that through our human instrumentality heaven has received some of its blessed angels. *Here* we may think that whatever is, is the best that a lapsed humanity will permit to be; but *there* we may realize that whatever is, is *right!*

Only one more thought before we lay down the pen from this work, the composition of which has been to its author productive of much happiness.

The great practical lesson that grows out of our consideration of the whole subject is full of important moral consequences, and it is this: — God formed us for heaven, — He has prepared heaven for us, — He continually desires to help us heavenwards, — by every operation of His providence He calls us to Himself, — He is willing to enable us to realize the commencement of the heavenly state even while we remain on earth, — He has so ordered it that this realization shall fill us with a perfect joy and a peace that abideth, — He has so constituted the human mind that its conceptions of Heaven shall be the most "glorious visions of the soul"; and that the cares of our lower life shall only force us to yearn for heaven with a longing that refuses to be extinguished, and with a hope that alone bears us up on its pinions above the weariness of time, — He has bound humanity together in this common nature, that, in view of the destiny of immortality, which is common to us all, we may love each other as brethren and help each other on in the way of our pilgrimage, — therefore, in all humility, and reliance upon our Saviour, the Lord Jesus Christ, we ought to strive to promote the fulfilment of the Divine purpose concerning us, and *hoping for Heaven* hereafter, we should LIVE FOR HEAVEN here.

Cambridge : Stereotyped and Printed by Welch, Bigelow, & Co.

www.ingramcontent.com/pod-product-compliance
Lightning Source LLC
LaVergne TN
LVHW011219110826
845150LV00006B/1481